MAXIMIZE YOUR READING

2

Maximize Your Reading 2

Copyright © 2017 by Pearson Education, Inc.

Pearson Education, Inc., 221 River Street, Hoboken, NJ 07030 USA

Staff credits: The people who made up the *Maximize Your Reading* team are Pietro Alongi, Rhea Banker, Tracey Munz Cataldo, Mindy DePalma, Gina DiLillo, Niki Lee, Amy McCormick, Lindsay Richman, and Paula Van Ells.

Text composition: MPS North America LLC
Design: EMC Design Ltd
Photo credits: Cover: Moodboard/Getty Images. Page 1: Max Tactic/Fotolia; 11 (bottom, left): Patrick Poendl/Fotolia; 11 (bottom, right): Arthur R./Fotolia; 11 (top): Leo Blanchette/Fotolia; 16 (bottom, left): Spuno/Fotolia; 16 (bottom, right): Michael Jung/Fotolia; 16 (center): Pixelspieler/Fotolia; 16 (top): Uwimages/Fotolia; 17: Paul Maguire/Shutterstock; 18: Visionsi/Fotolia; 19: Jean-Edouard Rozey/ Fotolia; 80 (bottom, left): Nazzalbe/Fotolia; 80 (bottom, right): S. Gatterwe/Fotolia; 80 (center): Monkey Business/Fotolia; 80 (top): Gorilla/Fotolia; 81: Calee Allen/Fotolia; 82: Dmitrijs Dmitrijevs/Fotolia; 83: Studio Damien Bert/Fotolia; 207: Mezzotint/Fotolia

ISBN-13: 978-0-13-466138-4   ISBN-10: 0-13-466138-9

Printed in the United States of America
2   16

pearsonelt.com/maximizeyourreading

CONTENTS

Reading Level 2 – Low Intermediate

Part 1   Comprehension Skills

Circle the letter of the correct answer.

1 Look at the picture in the article. What is the article about?

  a tigers in the wild

  b how tigers hunt

  c a mother tiger and her baby

  d a tiger cub being raised in captivity

2 Read the list below. What is the topic of the list?

  a desk

  b meeting

  c office

  d copy machine

  e computer

  f printer

  g paper

  h telephone

3 Read the passage. Is it a paragraph?

Technology is an important tool in education today. Many schools have computers and tablets in every classroom. There are many tablets on the market nowadays. The first computer was about 8 feet long and weighed 27 tons. Some schools are asking students to bring their own computers or tablets to class to cut costs.

a a paragraph
b not a paragraph

4 Read the passage. Choose the correct topic.

Nowadays, phones can do everything. They can tell you a joke, tell you when a storm is coming, or track how fast you do your morning run. The capabilities of mobile applications, or apps for short, continue to grow and expand. Many people have game apps on their mobile devices. You can play number or word games that make you think or just mindless games that help you pass the time. Other popular apps are the search tool apps. These help you find the answers you're looking for. In addition to these, social networking apps are popular, especially among young cell phone users. Teens all around the world only have to push a button to get connected to their friends. Other apps include sports apps, travel apps, and weather apps. People rely heavily on their apps for their everyday needs.

a mobile phones
b different kinds of apps
c using apps
d how to use an app on your phone

5 Read the passage. Choose the main idea.

During the month of September, when most colleges welcome a new group of incoming students, many of the teachers will be surprised at what they see. In the past few years, the number of college students between the ages of 40 and 64 has increased nearly 20%. There are now more than 2 million students in this age group enrolled in college. Many of these older students want to get higher pay, or get a better job after they get more education. There are some companies who will even pay their long-term employees to go back to school to get the up-to-date training being offered. Whatever the reason, there is an influx of older students and they are changing the face of college campuses across the United States.

a up-to-date training
b how to get into college
c older people going back to college
d college campuses across the United States

Part 2   Comprehension Skills

Read the passage. Then write the numbers of the sentences into the correct box.

Vacations are fun, but did you know that they have other benefits, also? Vacations are good for your health. When you take a vacation, you rest your mind and it decreases your blood pressure. Research shows that when you are on vacation, you get a better night's sleep. Taking time off helps develop your hobbies and interests, which can make you a happier, healthier person.

1 Research shows that when you are on vacation, you get a better night's sleep.
2 When you take a vacation, you rest your mind and it decreases your blood pressure.
3 Vacations are good for your health.
4 Taking time off helps develop your hobbies and interests, which can make you a happier, healthier person.

Main Idea	Supporting Details

Part 3 Comprehension Skills

Scan the information. Circle the letter of the correct answer.

Get up and Move!

Learn to dance like a professional.

Dance classes offered Mondays and Wednesday evenings from 6–8 p.m.
Town Hall: 895 Sycamore Avenue

Wear comfortable clothing and shoes.
No partner necessary!

Questions?
Call Maria Lennon at 555-2345

MOVING SALE

For sale: furniture, rugs, clothes, toys and books. Good prices! Everything must go! Rain or Shine!

Saturday, 7:00–11:00 am
109 Fable Court

Need help with the kids?

College student at home for the summer looking for babysitting jobs.

7 years of experience / Driver's license / References available.

Call Jane Doe at 555-9023
Email: jdoe@compway.com

Lost Dog!

Black and white, medium size, about 40 pounds. Name: Fluffy
If found, please call Joe Harris at 555-9908 or return to 6748 Willow Lane
Reward!

Grand Opening!

Come and have some fun at **Granville Sportsplex**
900 Tomkin Way

- **Exercise equipment**
- **Indoor soccer**
- **Outdoor tennis courts**
- **Free child care**
- **Basketball**
- **Indoor swimming pool**
- **Outdoor volleyball courts**
- **Memberships available!**

Call the manager, Kelly Keen at 555-9000

1 Where is the sale?
- **a** 895 Sycamore Avenue
- **b** 109 Fable Court
- **c** 6748 Willow Lane
- **d** 900 Tomkin Way

2 What is the babysitter's name?
- **a** Joe Harris
- **b** Maria Lennon
- **c** Jane Doe
- **d** Kelly Keen

Part 4 Comprehension Skills

Read the dialog. Circle the letter of the correct answer.

A: Welcome back, Mary!

B: Thanks, Kate.

A: So? Tell me all about it! How was it?

B: It was all right.

A: Just all right? You have to tell me more!

B: Well, we arrived on Sunday, and it was raining, so we didn't get to see the beautiful mountains that everyone talks about.

A: That's too bad. What about the next day?

B: Well, that's the thing. It never stopped!

A: Oh, I'm so sorry!

B: It's OK, we had a relaxing time anyway.

1 What are **A** and **B** talking about?
  a B's vacation
  b the mountains
  c the rain
  d work

2 What never stopped?
  a B's vacation
  b the mountains
  c the rain
  d the car

Part 5 Comprehension Skills

Read the paragraphs. Circle the letter of the pattern of organization for each paragraph.

1 Nowadays, phones can do everything. They can tell you a joke, tell you when a storm is coming, or track how fast you do your morning run. The capabilities of mobile applications, or apps for short, continue to grow and expand. Types of app that many people use on their mobile devices are game apps. You can play number or word games that make you think or just mindless games that help you pass the time. Other popular apps are search tool apps. These help you find the answers you're looking for. In addition to these, social networking apps are popular, especially among young cell phone users. Teens all around the world only have to push a button to get connected to their friends. Other apps include sports apps, travel apps, and weather apps. People rely heavily on their apps for their everyday needs.

   a comparison pattern
   b sequence pattern
   c listing pattern

2 Horses are beautiful animals. They can be intimidating to pet, however, since they are so large and powerful. There are certain steps you should take when petting a horse so that you and the horse feel comfortable with one another. First, open your hand and let the horse sniff you. This allows the horse to get a sense of you before you reach out to pet him. Once the horse has sniffed you, speak softly to him. While you are speaking, take the same hand that the horse sniffed and put it on the base of the neck. Next, gently stroke the horse's neck. Long strokes or pats are acceptable and make the horse happy. When you are patting the horse, talk to him again. Let him hear your voice. Finally, as you move away, let the horse smell your hand again. This helps the horse remember you for the next time you come to visit.

   a comparison pattern
   b sequence pattern
   c listing pattern

3 As costs for air travel continue to rise, more people are going back to the old-fashioned way of traveling by train. There are many ways these two modes of transportation differ. Airplanes take less time, but many travelers see the journey to the destination as part of their trip. They like to see the scenery along the way instead of flying over it. We know that airplanes get you to your destination faster and that trains can add several days to your trip. On a train, though, you are able to meet all sorts of interesting people, which can be a memorable part of your trip. Unlike the airplane, there is a certain romance to trains. People think of old black-and-white, romantic movies when they board a train. For these and other reasons, train travel is still alive today.

   a comparison pattern
   b sequence pattern
   c listing pattern

Part 6   Vocabulary Building

Read each question. Circle the letter of the correct answer.

1 What does the prefix *re-* in the word *retake* mean?

   a under

   b wrong

   c before

   d again

2 The suffix *-ly* changes the part of speech of a word. What part of speech is the word *legally*?

   a noun

   b verb

   c adjective

   d adverb

3 What is the root of the word *illegally*?

   a il

   b legal

   c ly

   d illegal

Part 7   Vocabulary Building

Circle the letter of the correct word or phrase.

1 The play was very _____ . We were all very _____ with the plot and characters.

   a amusing, amused

   b amused, amusing

2 Class is finished. Please _____ before you leave.

   a give the papers

   b hand in your papers

   c put the papers

Part 8   Vocabulary Building

Circle the letter of the word or phrase that has the same meaning as the underlined text.

1 Horses are beautiful animals. They can be <u>intimidating</u> to pet, however, since they are so large and powerful.

   a easy

   b frightening

   c hard

   d impossible

2 You can play number or word games that make you think or just mindless games that help you <u>pass the time</u>.

   a buy a watch

   b do something while time goes by

   c find out the time

   d look at the clock

Part 9   Vocabulary Building

Read the sentences. Write the subjects and the verbs in the correct box.

All of the pupils sat waiting patiently for the teacher.

From my window, I could see all of the beautiful sights of Rome.

Don't worry; the forecast called for sunshine.

Subjects	Verbs

Part 10   Vocabulary Building

Read the passage. Draw a circle around the subject pronouns, draw a box around the object pronouns, and underline the possessive adjectives.

My family loves animals. In fact we have over seven pets! First, there are our three

dogs—Fido, Spot, and Lady. My favorite is Lady. She is the oldest of the three dogs,

but she is still quick on her feet. She likes to run. Sometimes I throw a ball to her, but

she is not good at catching it. Fido and Spot can jump high and they often can catch

the balls I throw to them. I love watching that, especially when I throw them close by.

Next, we have four cats. Their names are Shadow, Skinny, Foxy, and Baby. Foxy looks

like a fox and that is why I named her that. I love all of my pets and I think they love

me, too.

Part 11   Vocabulary Building

Write the correct demonstrative adjective to complete each sentence.

These	This	that	those

1 Do you see _____ men over there? They are my brothers.

2 _____ bread is so good. Here, try some!

3 _____ houses on this side of the street are really beautiful.

4 I really like _____ store over there. It has nice clothing.

Part 12   Vocabulary Building

Read the sentences. Circle the correct referent for the underlined pronoun.

Fido and Spot can jump high and they often can catch the balls I throw to them. I love watching <u>that</u>!

a the fact that Fido and Spot can jump

b Fido and Spot catching the balls

c throwing the balls

Part 13   Language in Context

Read the passage. Then read each sentence. Circle the letter of the best meaning for the underlined word.

Your first year away at college can be exciting. Many first-time students live in college dormitories. These are also referred to as residence halls. In a residence hall, students share small rooms with one or two other students. There usually is a residence hall monitor for each floor of the building. This person makes sure that everyone is following the rules. The residence hall monitor also plans parties and activities for all of the students. There is always something going on. Dormitory life can be a lot of fun!

1 Many first-time students live in college <u>dormitories</u>.

  a beds

  b houses

  c classrooms

  d residence halls

2 There usually is a residence hall <u>monitor</u> for each floor of the building.

  a a person who makes sure people are following the rules

  b a person who talks a lot

  c a teacher

  d a person you share a room with

3 There usually is a residence hall monitor for each <u>floor</u> of the building.

  a carpet   **c** door

  b wood   **d** story

Part 14　Language in Context

Read the passage. Then complete each sentence with a word from the box by writing the correct word into the sentence.

Being in too many activities can have its downside. Children who are involved in too many activities can get burned out. They are running from activity to activity and they don't have time to just be kids. Oftentimes they are so tired at the end of the day that they can barely stay awake to do their homework and are not getting enough sleep. When this starts to happen, you know that your child needs to cut back. Encourage him or her to cut down the number of activities and focus on one or two that he or she really loves.

involved	cut back	burned out
downside	barely	cut down

1 If you do something too often you can get _____ and you won't want to do it anymore.

2 Frank needs to _____ on eating sweets. He is overweight and is not healthy.

3 I _____ know her. I don't feel comfortable asking her to lend me her book.

4 There are pros and cons for everything. You just need to decide if you can handle the _____ of something.

5 If you want to make a change, get _____ in a local charity organization.

6 This essay is way too long. Read it again and _____ the number of words so it is no longer than 500 words.

Previewing and Predicting

PREVIEWING

Presentation

Previewing

Previewing means to look at a text quickly before you read it. Looking at the pictures, titles, subtitles, graphics, and words in bold print can give you clues on what the text is about. This information helps you understand the text before you read it.

Practice 1

Look at the picture and read the title of the book. What do you think the book is about? Circle the letter of the correct answer.

1 This book is about

   a the other things that Leonardo DaVinci was good at.

   b Leonardo DaVinci's paintings.

   c how Leonardo DaVinci became a painter.

2 This book is about

   a trying to remember your past.

   b playing games that help you remember your childhood.

   c mental exercises that improve how well you remember things.

3 This book is about

   a learning how to ice climb.

   b the dangers of ice climbing.

   c the best places to ice climb.

4 This book is about

   a how to travel to the French Riviera.

   b learning how to speak French.

   c day trips you can take on the French Riviera.

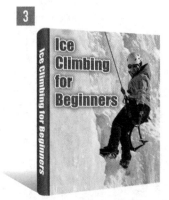

Previewing

Previewing is when you look at a text quickly before you read it. It helps you know what the reading is about so you can decide:

- which articles to read in a magazine or newspaper.
- whether the book is interesting and you want to read it.

Previewing can help you with understanding the reading, too. You get some ideas about the reading when you preview. Your brain is already thinking about the topic when you start to read, and this helps you understand more and read faster.

It is good to preview readings for school, but it can also help you with any kind of reading. Ask yourself these questions when you preview:

- What is it? (What type of reading is it? Look at the layout of the text and the information given. Is it fiction, nonfiction, a newspaper article, an email message, a letter, or an advertisement?)
- Who wrote it, and who is it written for?
- What is it about?
- How long is it?
- Is it difficult or easy to read?
- Is it interesting or useful to you?
- What will come next in the reading?

Practice 2

Part 1

Preview the text. Then read the question and circle the letter of the correct answer.

1 What is this text?
  a a letter
  b an advertisement
  c a test
  d an email

2 Who wrote it?
  a teachers
  b parents
  c students
  d principal

3 What will come next in the text?
  a the date of the dance
  b the time of the dance
  c instructions on how to dance
  d information on different kinds of dances

School Dance

Cary High School Gymnasium

Organized by the
Student Social Club

Saturday, October 23, 2013

Join us in the evening at

Part 2

Preview the text. Then read the question and circle the letter of the correct answer.

4 What is this text?

    a a paragraph in a book

    b a letter

    c an email

    d an advertisement

Re: Change meeting date

Joe,

I cannot meet on Tuesday to discuss the sales reports. I have another meeting at that time with a customer. Can we reschedule for next

5 Who wrote it?

    a a teacher

    b a co-worker

    c a friend

    d a family member

6 What will come next in the text?

    a a topic

    b a meeting place

    c a day

    d a time

Part 3

Preview the text. Then read the question and circle the letter of the correct answer.

7 What is this text?

    a an article

    b an email

    c a letter

    d an advertisement

Hi Katie!

It was so good to see you the other day! I had a great time at my birthday party. I was very surprised! Thank you for the flowers. They were

8 Who wrote it?

    a a friend

    b a boss

    c a salesperson

    d a teacher

9 What will come next in the text?

    a information about a garden

    b details about the presents she received

    c description of the flowers

    d other guests at the party

Practice 3

Part 1

Preview the graphs for the brochure. Circle the letter of the correct answer.

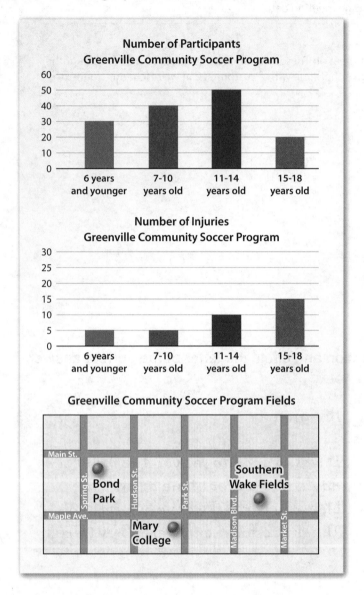

What is this brochure about?

a soccer schedule information

b information about the soccer coaches

c how to play soccer

d the soccer program in Greenville

e information about the tennis program in Greenville

Part 2

Preview the table of contents for the book. Circle the letter of the correct answer.

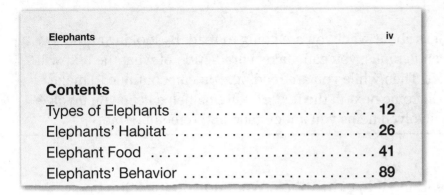

Elephants   iv

Contents

What is this book about?

a how to feed elephants

b the interaction between elephants and giraffes

c animal habitats

d elephants

Part 3

Preview the table of contents for the book. Circle the letter of the correct answer.

Puerto Rico   iv

Contents

Who is this book for?

a people who live in Puerto Rico

b people who want to visit Puerto Rico

c people who want to learn Spanish

d people who like to travel

PREDICTING

Predicting

Predicting is making a guess about what you are going to read. By looking at the pictures, titles, subtitles, and graphs, you can make a prediction of what the text will be about before you read it. Then while you are reading, you can continue to make predictions about what will come next in the text. Predicting helps keep you involved in the reading, and being involved helps you understand and remember more.

Practice 1

Look at the picture and read the title of the book. What do you think the book is about? Circle the letter of the correct answer.

1 This book is about
   a colleges around the country.
   b how to apply to college programs.
   c learning how to get better test scores for college.
   d learning about which college is better for you.

2 This book is about
   a how to pour wine.
   b how to tell if a wine is good.
   c different types of French wine.
   d the process of making wine.

3 This book is about
   a how to give a great speech.
   b various speeches remembered over the years.
   c Martin Luther King's speech, "I have a dream…."
   d the history of speech making.

4 This book is about
   a jokes from different countries.
   b jokes for any event or situation.
   c how to write a joke.
   d famous comedians.

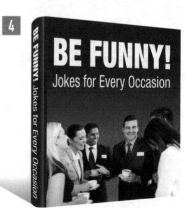

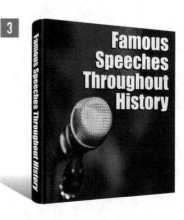

Practice 2

Part 1

Look at the picture and read the title of the magazine article. What do you think the article is about? Write the letter of each description in the correct box.

a finding a small apartment

b traveling in outer space

c how to organize your apartment

d ideas on how to live comfortably in a small apartment

e how to make your apartment bigger

f how to maximize the space in your apartment

g putting more things in your small apartment

h difficulties of living in a small apartment

Ideas in the article	Ideas not in the article

Part 2

Look at the picture and read the title of the magazine article. What do you think the article is about? Write the letter of each description in the correct box.

a farmland in the United States

b how many hours in a day

c daily schedule of a farmer

d jobs of a farmer

e daily activities of a farmer

f how farm life compares to city life

g what a farmer does to relax

h animals on a farm

Ideas in the article	Ideas not in the article

Part 3

Look at the picture and read the title of the magazine article. What do you think the article is about? Write the letter of each description in the correct box.

A Disappearing Species: Help Save the Red Wolf

a   how red wolves are different from gray wolves

b   reasons why red wolves are decreasing in numbers

c   the definition of species

d   the dangers of red wolves

e   how we can help save the red wolf

f   areas where red wolves live

g   what is endangering the red wolf

h   how to make a red wolf disappear

Ideas in the article	Ideas not in the article

Practice 3

Read the chapter title and heading. Circle the letter of the topic for each section.

1 This section is about
   a soccer and baseball.
   b games you play at a party.
   c games you play outside.
   d games you play inside.

2 This section is about
   a different kinds of calendars.
   b making a schedule for your day.
   c skills management.
   d activities during your day.

3 This section is about
   a holidays.
   b different cultures.
   c birthday parties.
   d celebrations in Asia.

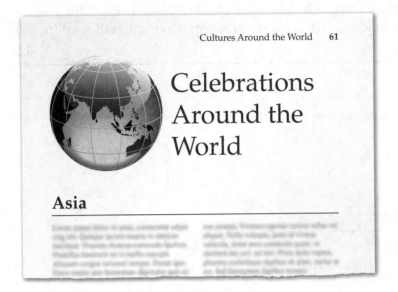

Cultures Around the World   61

Celebrations Around the World

Asia

4 This section is about
   a modern jobs.
   b jobs within the computer industry.
   c fixing a computer.
   d learning how to use the computer.

Modern Jobs   61

The Computer Industry

Jobs

COMBINED SKILLS: PREVIEWING AND PREDICTING

Presentation

Previewing and Predicting

Previewing is one of the first steps to making a prediction. First, preview the pictures, titles, subtitles, and graphs to get an idea as to what the text is about. Then, after you have an idea of what you will be reading, make predictions on what you will read in the text.

Practice 1

Read the Table of Contents and answer the question.

Save Our Planet iv

Contents

1 In which chapter will you read about the following idea?

Fill plastic water bottles with water and use them again.

a Chapter 5

b Chapter 3

c Chapter 1

d Chapter 6

2 In which chapter will you read about the following idea?

Clean up the parks around your city.

a Chapter 4

b Chapter 3

c Chapter 2

d Chapter 7

3 In which chapter will you read about the following idea?

Do not buy things from a store.
 a Chapter 1
 b Chapter 8
 c Chapter 4
 d Chapter 6

4 In which chapter will you read about the following idea?

Grow organic vegetables in your own garden.
 a Chapter 7
 b Chapter 4
 c Chapter 2
 d Chapter 3

5 In which chapter will you read about the following idea?

Turn the lights off in the rooms you are not using.
 a Chapter 8
 b Chapter 1
 c Chapter 5
 d Chapter 2

6 In which chapter will you read about the following idea?

Ride to work with a co-worker.
 a Chapter 2
 b Chapter 8
 c Chapter 1
 d Chapter 5

7 In which chapter will you read about the following idea?

Take your newspapers and bottles to a recycling center.
 a Chapter 2
 b Chapter 6
 c Chapter 4
 d Chapter 3

8 In which chapter will you read about the following idea?

Find the contact information for the Environmental Protection Agency in the United States.
 a Chapter 2
 b Chapter 7
 c Chapter 8
 d Chapter 4

Practice 2

Part 1

Look at the graphs for this brochure. What information can be found in this brochure? Circle the letters of all that apply.

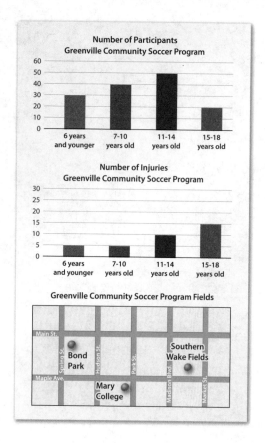

a the number of injuries in the soccer program

b the ages of soccer players in the Greenville program

c the differences between football and soccer

d directions to the soccer fields

e the number of players in the soccer program

f the soccer schedules for the year

g information on the baseball program in Greenville

h how to play soccer

i information on the coaches

Part 2

Look at the Table of Contents for this book. What information can be found in this book? Circle the letters of all that apply.

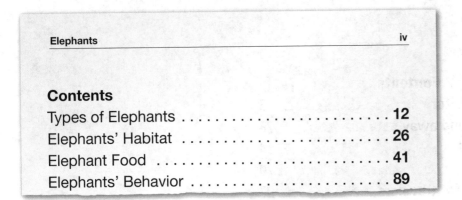

Elephants   iv

Contents

a information about the African elephant

b information about an elephant's home

c information about what an elephant eats

d information about how elephants interact with one another

e information about how elephants differ from giraffes

f information about elephants in zoos

g information about why elephants are endangered

Part 3

Look at the Table of Contents for this book. What information can be found in this book? Circle the letters of all that apply.

Puerto Rico   iv

Contents

a information about the history of Puerto Rico

b information on how to get to Puerto Rico

c information about transportation options within Puerto Rico

d useful phrases and words in Spanish

e activities you can do in Puerto Rico

f documentation you need to visit Puerto Rico

g information on English words to use in Puerto Rico

h information on the other Caribbean Islands

Identifying Topics, Main Ideas, and Details
IDENTIFYING THE TOPIC OF A LIST

Presentation

Identifying the Topic of a List

Look at the words in the list. What does each word have in common? The thing that is in common is usually the topic of the list.

Practice 1

Circle the letter of the topic in each list.

1
a carrot
b cucumber
c green pepper
d mushroom
e vegetable
f tomato
g corn

2
a bathroom
b kitchen
c living room
d attic
e basement
f house
g bedroom

3
a Spain
b Germany
c China
d Country
e Indonesia
f Brazil
g Colombia

4
a worried
b sad
c emotion
d happy
e excited
f bored
g scared

5
a menu
b waiter
c table
d food
e drink
f bill
g restaurant

6
a suitcase
b ticket
c map
d trip
e clothes
f money
g camera

Practice 2

Draw a line to match the list of words to its topic.

1 word, definition, pronunciation, guide, word, part of speech   education

2 beef, fish, chicken, pork, lamb   meat

3 subject, teacher, test, homework, grade, classroom   town

4 milk, lemonade, water, tea, juice, wine   beverage

5 library, police station, grocery store, gas station, fire station, park   dictionary

6 root, petal, stem, flower, leaf   plant

UNDERSTANDING PARAGRAPHS

Understanding Paragraphs

A paragraph is a group of sentences about the same topic. The beginning of the paragraph has a sentence that states the topic. All of the other sentences in the paragraph are about the same topic.

Practice 1

Read each passage. Then decide whether it is or is not a paragraph. Circle the letter of your answer.

1 Have you ever heard a buzzing sound and then seen a flash of something zoom by? Most likely it was a hummingbird. Hummingbirds are the fastest of all birds. Their wings flap between 12 and 80 times per second. These wings allow them to change direction quickly. Chances are you won't see one for long. In a second, they are gone!

    a a paragraph
    b not a paragraph

2 There are many fast-food chain restaurants in the United States. They sell hamburgers, fried chicken, and French fries. Eating healthy is important. Fruits and vegetables are the key to a healthy diet. Ice cream is a favorite dessert for many people. In some areas of the United States, there are ice-cream trucks that go through neighborhoods selling ice cream.

    a a paragraph
    b not a paragraph

3 If you have an animal, then you know that finding a good veterinarian is important. A veterinarian is a doctor who specializes in the treatment of animals. There are three types of veterinarians. There are some who take care of large animals, such as horses, cows, and sheep. Other veterinarians take care of small animals, such as cats and dogs. The last type of veterinarian takes care of exotic animals, such as snakes, lizards, and zoo animals. Each type of veterinarian is important for the well-being of all types of animals.

    a a paragraph
    b not a paragraph

4 How do you get to work every day? The price of public transportation varies greatly in different cities. Many people like to ride their bikes to work. Cities have laws for sharing the road with bikers. Carpooling is a great way to save money and gas. Some companies allow their employees to work at home so that they do not have to commute to work every day.

    a a paragraph
    b not a paragraph

5 Your first year away at college can be exciting. Many first-time students live in college dormitories. These are also referred to as residence halls. In a residence hall, students share small rooms with one or two other students. There usually is a residence hall monitor for each floor of the building. This person makes sure that everyone is following the rules. The residence hall monitor also plans parties and activities for all of the students. There is always something going on. Dormitory life can be a lot of fun!

a a paragraph

b not a paragraph

Practice 2

Read the passage. Decide if it is a paragraph. Circle the letter of the correct answer.

1 Many holidays are celebrated in the United States. Kwanzaa is a special holiday celebrated by African Americans. This holiday began in Los Angeles in 1966. Maulana Karenza, the creator of this holiday, believes in family and remembering African traditions. The holiday of Kwanzaa helps keep African traditions alive for African Americans.

a a paragraph

b not a paragraph

2 Having a pet can be a wonderful experience. There are over 78 million pet dogs in the United States. Birds often fly to warmer areas in the winter months. Pets can cost a lot of money. A veterinarian is a doctor who treats animals.

a a paragraph

b not a paragraph

3 What is your favorite type of sweet? Chocolate is a very popular dessert option. There are many kinds of chocolate. Sweet, milk, semi-sweet, unsweetened, and cocoa powder are just a few. All chocolate is made from roasted and ground cocoa beans. You can cook and bake with chocolate, but most people like to just eat it straight from the package!

a a paragraph

b not a paragraph

4 If you have trouble focusing during the day, chances are you are not getting enough sleep. Doctors recommend that people get 7–9 hours of sleep per night. If you have difficulty sleeping, setting up a bedtime routine can help. Begin with reading or watching a particular TV show, and then after it is over, turn out the lights and go to sleep. Sleep helps you stay healthy both physically and mentally.

a a paragraph

b not a paragraph

5 Between May and September, people living along the Atlantic Coast prepare for hurricane season. Tornadoes are spiraling wind storms that can cause a lot of damage. It is estimated that 63,000 people die from an earthquake each year.

a a paragraph

b not a paragraph

Practice 3

Part 1

Read the paragraph. Then write the number of each sentence in the correct box on p. 31.

Mark Twain

Mark Twain was a famous writer of novels, including two about young boys named Tom Sawyer and Huckleberry Finn. Mark Twain was not the author's real name. His real name was Samuel Clemens. Clemens was born in 1835, in Missouri. When he was four years old, Clemens's family moved to the town of Hannibal, Missouri. This area became the inspiration for his famous novels. Almost two centuries later, Mark Twain is still a well-known author whose novels are enjoyed by children and adults around the world.

1. When he was four years old, Clemens's family moved to the town of Hannibal, Missouri.
2. This area became the inspiration for his famous novels.
3. Mark Twain was not the author's real name.
4. His real name was Samuel Clemens.
5. Clemens was born in 1835, in Missouri.
6. Almost two centuries later, Mark Twain is still a well-known author whose novels are enjoyed by children and adults around the world.
7. Mark Twain was a famous writer of novels, including two about young boys named Tom Sawyer and Huckleberry Finn.

Topic Sentence	Body Sentences	Concluding Sentence

Part 2

Read the paragraph. Then write the number of each sentence in the correct box.

Vegetarian

A vegetarian is someone who does not eat meat, and there are many reasons why people become vegetarians. Some people simply do not like the taste of meat. Others believe it is cruel to eat meat from an animal. Then there are some people whose religion does not allow them to eat meat. There are also some people who think it is unhealthy to eat meat. Vegetarians eat a lot of vegetables, fruits, beans, and soy products (such as tofu). Whatever the reason, the number of vegetarians is increasing all over the world.

1 There are also some people who think it is unhealthy to eat meat.

2 Whatever the reason, the number of vegetarians is increasing all over the world.

3 Then there are some people whose religion does not allow them to eat meat.

4 A vegetarian is someone who does not eat meat, and there are many reasons why people become vegetarians.

5 Some people simply do not like the taste of meat.

6 Vegetarians eat a lot of vegetables, fruits, beans, and soy products (such as tofu).

7 Others believe it is cruel to eat meat from an animal.

Topic Sentence	Body Sentences	Concluding Sentence

Part 3

Read the paragraph. Then write the number of each sentence in the correct box.

Roommates

Jake and John are roommates, but they are very different people. Jake gets up at dawn, while John sleeps in every morning until 10 A.M. Jake works hard all day around the house, while John lazes around the house, reading and watching television. Jake cooks all of his own meals with fresh ingredients, but John goes to fast-food restaurants or orders pizza every night. Despite their many differences, Jake and John are good friends, and they like living together.

1 Jake and John are roommates, but they are very different people.

2 Jake cooks all of his own meals with fresh ingredients, but John goes to fast-food restaurants or orders pizza every night.

3 Despite their many differences, Jake and John are good friends, and they like living together.

4 Jake gets up at dawn, while John sleeps in every morning until 10 A.M.

5 Jake works hard all day around the house, while John lazes around the house, reading and watching television.

Topic Sentence	Body Sentences	Concluding Sentence

IDENTIFYING THE TOPIC OF A PARAGRAPH

> ## Presentation
> **Identifying the Topic of a Paragraph**
> The topic is what the paragraph is about. One way to find the topic of a paragraph is to look for a word or phrase that is repeated often in the sentences. That word or phrase is the topic.

Practice 1

Read each paragraph. Circle the letter of the correct topic.

1 What do you see when you look at the moon? The dark spots on the moon represent different things in different countries. In the United States, people think the shapes look like a man's face. That is how we got the expression "the man on the moon." People in other parts of the world say that these spots make a picture of a rabbit. Others see a woman reading a book. There are many images and stories of the shapes on the moon.

The topic of the paragraph is
a how Earth rotates around the moon.
b how man first walked on the moon.
c the depth of the craters on the moon.
d the images people see on the moon.

2 Lightning in the sky can be so beautiful. How is lightning created? When a bolt of lightning flashes across the sky, you are seeing a giant electrical spark. During storms, electricity builds up in rain clouds. Once in a while, this electricity must find a place to go, so it forms a bolt of electricity called a lightning bolt.

The topic of the paragraph is
a how lightning is formed.
b the dangers of electricity.
c tips to stay safe in an electrical storm.
d electricity.

3 Thanks to two French brothers, Jacques and Joseph Montgolfier, the world has an interesting mode of transportation—the hot air balloon. After lunch one day, the brothers threw their paper bag into the fireplace. Before it burned, the bag filled with smoke and hot air. The brothers watched in amazement as the bag rose up the chimney. This gave them an idea to make more balloons, and eventually they created the very first hot air balloon.

The topic of the paragraph is
a the science behind the hot air balloon.
b how hot air balloons were created.
c how to travel by hot air balloon.
d interesting modes of transportation.

4 Everybody loves popcorn! People have munched on popcorn for thousands of years. Scientists found popped kernels of corn that are more than 5,000 years old. When Christopher Columbus landed in the Americas, he saw Native Americans eating popcorn. He also saw them stringing kernels together to wear as necklaces and hair decorations. Popcorn was popular then, and it is still popular today.

The topic of the paragraph is
a Native Americans.
b the history of popcorn.
c how to make popcorn.
d crafts you can make from popcorn.

Practice 2

Read each paragraph. Circle the letter of the correct topic.

1 Today, there are many activities for children to be involved in. Many of these activities are both educational and fun. They can help children develop their talents and learn new skills. Activities can provide opportunities to learn important life skills, such as discipline and teamwork. Many activities can help kids meet other kids outside of school. Some activities can also help kids stay physically fit. There is a lot to gain from doing activities.

The topic of the paragraph is
a how to develop a child's talent.
b important life skills.
c meeting friends.
d the benefits of activities.

2 Being in too many activities can have downsides. Children who are involved in too many activities can get burned out. They are running from activity to activity, and they don't have time to just be kids. Often, they are so tired at the end of the day that they can barely stay awake to do their homework and are not getting enough sleep. When this starts to happen, you know that your child needs to cut back.

The topic of the paragraph is
a the problems of being too involved.
b sleeping problems.
c kids who have problems with their homework.
d sick and tired children.

3 So how do you cut back on all your child does in life? The problem can be that all of the activities are interesting to your child. One thing to do before getting involved is to think carefully about the activity and decide whether or not this is something your child really wants to do. Also, ask yourself these questions: Is my child's plate already full? Will this affect my child's schoolwork? Is my child truly interested in this activity? These questions will help you decide whether taking on this new activity is the right decision.

The topic of the paragraph is
a problems with children.
b how to ask questions.
c feeding your child.
d questions to help you make decisions.

4 If you find that your child likes all of the activities, then it may be a question of scheduling his/her time so that he/she is more productive. Look at everything your child is doing during the day and see if he/she can spend time more wisely. For example, can your child do his/her homework in the car on the way to these activities? Does he/she spend time watching television or playing video games? If so, this can easily be something to cut back on.

The topic of the paragraph is
a scheduling and being more productive.
b driving to activities.
c helping your child with homework.
d cutting back on television and video games.

IDENTIFYING THE MAIN IDEA

Presentation

Identifying the Main Idea
The main idea is the most important point about the topic. To find the main idea, first find the topic and then ask, "What does the author want me to know about this topic?" The answer to that question is the main idea. The main idea can be found in one sentence. This sentence is called a "topic sentence."

Practice 1

Read each paragraph. Circle the letter of the statement that describes the main idea.

You hear of people running marathons all the time, but have you ever heard of an ultramarathon? In an ultramarathon, athletes run 30 miles or more. They run through cities, over rough trails, and through forests. Some of these races are 100 miles long! An average time for a 100-mile ultramarathon is 25 hours, but the world record is 11 hours! To be an ultramarathoner, you have to really love to run!

1 a Ultramarathoners love to run.
 b Ultramarathons are races through forests and cities.
 c Ultramarathons are over 100 miles long.
 d Ultramarathons are races over 30 miles.

There are some people whose mood is affected by the grey skies during the winter months. These people have seasonal affective disorder. Seasonal affective disorder, or SAD for short, is a mood disorder. Some SAD patients experience feelings of sadness or depression, while others experience physical symptoms, such as headaches or stomachaches. There are many treatments for this disorder. Light therapy is a common treatment. The patients sit under a bright light that mimics the sun. After 30–60 minutes, the patients feel much better.

2 **a** SAD patients experience sadness and headaches.
    b Seasonal affective disorder is a mood disorder.
    c People with SAD sit under bright lights.
    d Many places have grey skies in winter time.

Do you remember your dreams? Many people believe that dreams can help us figure out our problems in life. If you are having difficulty sleeping and you can't figure out why, put a notebook and a pencil near your bed. If you wake up in the middle of a dream, write what you remember in the notebook. After a few weeks, you may see a pattern in your dreams, and these patterns may help you figure out what is bothering you.

3 **a** Write your dreams down.
    b Our dreams can help us figure out our problems in life.
    c Ideas for helping you sleep.
    d Put a notebook by your bed at night.

There are many challenging times when raising a child. Some parents hire professionals to help with these challenges. From homework help to toilet training, there is a service for any problem a parent needs help with. One recent survey showed that there has been a 50 percent increase in parent-help services. Some child psychologists believe this could be hurtful to the parent-child relationship, while others believe that helping parents avoid the typical arguments with their children can strengthen this relationship. Either way, if you need help, there is always someone you can turn to for help.

4 **a** Parents can hire professionals to help with challenges.
    b Raising a child can be difficult.
    c Parent-help services have increased over the years.
    d It is better to help your own child.

Practice 2

Read the essay. Underline the sentence in each paragraph that gives you the main idea.

1 We love our pet dogs, cats, and horses. But these animals can do more than just love us back; they can help us in many ways. Animals that help others are called service animals. These animals help people do tasks that they would not be able to do alone. Service animals are not pets but working animals doing a job. Laws state that they can go anywhere a human can go if they are helping a human.

2 There are many kinds of service animals. The most common service animals are guide dogs. Guide dogs help people who cannot see well. Some puppies are raised for the purpose of becoming guide dogs. Puppies spend their first year with a family who helps them become socialized and prepares them for later training. At about 18 months of age, guide dogs get special training. This training takes about three to six months. They learn to wear a harness, walk on crowded streets, stop at curbs, and protect their human partners.

3 Hearing dogs are dogs that help people who don't hear well. These dogs are trained to alert their human partners to ordinary sounds, such as alarm clocks, a baby's cry, the ring of a telephone, or a door bell. They are also trained to listen for sounds of danger, such as fire alarms or the sounds of intruders in a house. These hearing dogs usually alert their human partner by touching the partner with a paw and then leading them to the source of the sound.

4 Some dogs, and other animals, such as cats and horses, are therapeutic companions. These animals provide emotional support for people who are sick, depressed, or lonely. These animals get special training for staying by their human partner's side. They bring much-welcomed companionship and joy to patients of all ages.

5 Dogs, cats, and horses are not the only animals that help humans with disabilities. The Capuchin monkey can help people who are paralyzed or have other problems with walking or moving. These monkeys are very smart and can perform essential tasks, such as turning lights on and off and picking up dropped objects. These monkeys make a big difference in their companions' lives.

6 The organizations that train these service animals also make sure that they are leading rewarding, enjoyable, healthy lives. They check in with the animals often to be sure that the partnership is a good fit for both the animal and the human. And, when the animal gets too old to work anymore, the organization makes sure it has a good home to go to after retirement.

Identifying the Main Idea

The main idea is the most important point about the topic. To find the main idea, first find the topic and then ask, "What does the author want me to know about this topic?" The answer to that question is the main idea. The main idea can be found in one sentence. This sentence is called a "topic sentence."

The main idea gives you a more complete understanding of the topic. However, for any topic, different main ideas are possible. Some can be too specific, or too general. It is important to read the whole paragraph and decide which main idea is the best.

Ask yourself these questions:

Specific: Does this sentence go into too much detail about one part of the main idea?

General: Is this sentence too general? Does it go into enough detail about the main idea?

Practice 3

Read the paragraph below. Write the letter of the idea on the correct line.

1 There is nothing like a cold glass of water on a hot day. Water is not only refreshing; it is imperative for our survival. Seventy-one percent of Earth's surface is covered with water, but only a small percentage is safe to drink. Most of the water on Earth is salty. Humans who drink salt water will eventually die. Crops will also die if they are watered with salt water. Industries cannot use salt water in most situations, either. It will cause their machinery to rust more quickly and not work properly. We need fresh water to survive and for crops and companies to thrive.

a Water is important for our survival.

b Water is good for us.

c Seventy-one percent of Earth's surface is covered with water.

Main Idea _____

Too Specific _____

Too General _____

Read the paragraph below. Write the letter of the idea on the correct line.

2 For thousands of years, people have used the power of the sun to turn salt water into fresh water. The sun naturally draws water upward in the form of water vapor. As the water vapor rises, the salt is left behind. If the water vapor is captured, it turns to water droplets. These water droplets may taste a little salty, but they are safe to drink.

a The sun helps us.

b The sun draws water upward.

c The sun can turn salt water into fresh water.

Main Idea _____

Too Specific _____

Too General _____

IDENTIFYING SUPPORTING DETAILS

Presentation

Identifying Supporting Details

Besides the topic and main idea, a paragraph also includes facts and ideas that support the main idea. These supporting sentences give us more information about the main idea. They can be facts, examples, explanations, reasons, or descriptions of the topic. They tell us who, what, when, where, why, how, how much, or how many.

Look at the paragraph below. The sentence in boldface is the main idea. The underlined sentences are the supporting details.

I had a terrible vacation. <u>First, I got sick.</u> I had a sore throat and a fever all week. <u>Second, the shower in my room wasn't working.</u> The water came out cold! <u>Also, it was rainy.</u> We didn't see the sun all week long. It was a miserable time.

Practice 1

Part 1

Read the sentences. Write the number of each sentence in the correct box.

1 My sister Tracy is one of the kindest people I know.
2 Tracy reads to sick people who are in the hospital.
3 After school, she tutors students who are having trouble.
4 She volunteers in a homeless shelter every Saturday morning.

Main Idea	Supporting Details

Part 2

Read the sentences. Write the number of each sentence in the correct box.

1 I am taking a cooking class.
2 The instructor is from Louisiana.
3 The food is spicy but very good.
4 We are learning how to cook Cajun-style dishes.

Main Idea	Supporting Details

Part 3

Read the sentences. Write the number of each sentence in the correct box.

1 It is not an expensive sport, since you can walk anywhere.
2 Walking helps you lose weight and keeps your heart healthy.
3 Walking is an excellent way to stay healthy.
4 You can walk and talk with friends.

Main Idea	Supporting Details

Part 4

Read the sentences. Write the number of each sentence in the correct box.

1 I love my new part-time job at the coffee shop.
2 I like to make the coffee and talk with the customers.
3 I get to drink free coffee, too!
4 It is easy and fun.

Main Idea	Supporting Details

Part 5

Read the sentences. Write the number of each sentence in the correct box.

1 Other times, I meet a nice person, and we talk the whole way to work.
2 When I'm tired, I can sleep on the bus.
3 Sometimes, I read and do my homework on the bus.
4 The bus is a great way to get to work.

Main Idea	Supporting Details

Practice 2

Read the paragraphs. Underline the supporting sentences in each.

1 My teacher makes class lots of fun. He creates games and activities to help us to review the material we learn in class. He lets us work in groups. I like working with my friends. We also take a lot of field trips. We go to museums and places around town to learn more about the subjects we read about in class. He is a great teacher.

2 There are many types of superstitions in every culture. Some superstitions relate to animals. A black cat that passes your path is believed to be bad luck, while a rabbit's foot can bring you good luck. Others have to do with things. Walking under ladders, splitting wishbones, and breaking mirrors are popular superstitions. Some people believe you will have seven years' bad luck if you break a mirror. Certain numbers and calendar days are superstitious for some people. Friday the 13th is such a feared day that some people don't leave their house! There are many things out there to give you a fright!

3 Driving is a big responsibility, but unfortunately there are many things in the car that can distract us. Other passengers, especially children, can be very distracting to our driving. If they are asking you questions or to help them with something, you take your mind off the road. Another big distraction is your cell phone. If your phone rings or a text comes in, you are tempted to respond it. It is better to keep your cell phone in the back seat where you can't get to it while driving. Food can also be a distraction. If you drop some food while driving, you are tempted to pick it up, and this takes your mind and eyes off the road. Driving safely is probably the most important thing you can do every day.

4 There are many kinds of spicy foods around the world. Food from Thailand is known to be very spicy. The Thai people use Bird's Eye chili peppers in many dishes. This chili pepper is the main reason why Thai cuisine is known for its spiciness. Food from Sichuan province in China is some of the spiciest in the world. Before you try a spoonful of Sichuan Hot-Pot, make sure you have a towel around to wipe your face! In India, they make some very spicy foods. Vindaloo Pork has a very hot curry sauce that will definitely make you reach for some water! If you like spicy food, you can eat your way around the world.

Scanning

SCANNING FOR KEY WORDS AND PHRASES

Scanning for the Key Word

Scanning is a very fast kind of reading. You scan when you want to find information quickly. We usually scan for specific information, such as words, numbers, and dates.

When you scan, your eyes move very quickly over the page. You don't read all of the words on the page; you only look for the words that will help you find the information you need. Before you scan, think about the information you are looking for. For example, if you are looking for a date, scan for numbers on the page.

Practice 1

Read the list of words. Circle the letters next to the key word.

1 Circle the letters next to the word *had*.
- **a** had
- **b** have
- **c** had
- **d** hat
- **e** heard
- **f** had
- **g** has
- **h** hand

2 Circle the letters next to the word *were*.
- **a** was
- **b** why
- **c** where
- **d** were
- **e** with
- **f** were
- **g** way
- **h** were

3 Circle the letters next to the word *first*.
- **a** free
- **b** first
- **c** for
- **d** first
- **e** fire
- **f** fast
- **g** first
- **h** far

4 Circle the letters next to the word *there*.
- **a** there
- **b** three
- **c** through
- **d** there
- **e** theme
- **f** them
- **g** there
- **h** their

5 Circle the letters next to the word *last*.

   a later

   b last

   c look

   d last

   e lame

   f last

   g laugh

   h land

6 Circle the letters next to the word *every*.

   a every

   b even

   c ear

   d each

   e every

   f either

   g every

   h ever

7 Circle the letters next to the word *thought*.

   a through

   b there

   c thought

   d though

   e then

   f thought

   g thought

   h thorough

8 Circle the letters next to the word *best*.

   a best

   b beat

   c beet

   d bent

   e best

   f bet

   g better

   h best

Presentation

Scanning for the Key Phrase

Scanning is a very fast kind of reading. You scan when you want to find information quickly. We usually scan for specific information, such as words, numbers, and dates.

When you scan, your eyes move very quickly over the page. You don't read all of the words on the page; you only look for the words that will help you find the information you need. Before you scan, think about the information you are looking for. For example, if you are looking for a date, scan for numbers on the page.

Practice 2

Read the list of words. Circle the letters next to the key phrase.

1 Circle the letters next to the phrase *hand in*.

   a hand in

   b hand over

   c hand out

   d hand in

   e hand in

   f have on

   g hang up

   h hand in

2 Circle the letters next to the phrase *look after*.

   a look after

   b look out

   c look in

   d look after

   e look after

   f look over

   g look up

   h look after

3 Circle the letters next to the phrase *call on*.

a call on
b call in
c call on
d call out
e call over
f call on
g call off
h call on

4 Circle the letters next to the phrase *check out*.

a check in
b check into
c check out
d check up
e check out
f check up
g check out
h check out

5 Circle the letters next to the phrase *get back*.

a get back
b get over
c get off
d get back
e get on
f get back
g get out
h get back

6 Circle the letters next to the phrase *take out*.

a take over
b take out
c take in
d take out
e take on
f take out
g take out
h take back

Presentation

Scanning for the Key Words and Phrases in a Paragraph
When you are scanning for information in a paragraph or story, remember that you are not reading to comprehend the information. You are just looking for a key word or phrase. Just look for the key words as quickly as you can. Later, you will read the passage and think about what it means.

Practice 3

Scan the paragraph. Look for the exact key word or phrase, and count how many times it appears in each paragraph. Circle the letter of the number of times.

1 Key word: *dreams*

Do you remember your dreams? Many people believe that dreams can help us figure out our problems in life. If you are having difficulty sleeping but you can't figure out why, put a notebook and a pencil near your bed. If you wake up in the middle of a dream, write what you remember in the notebook. After a few weeks, you may see a pattern in your dreams, and these patterns may help you figure out what is bothering you.

a two   **c** four
b three   **d** five

2 Key phrase: *service animals*

We love our pet dogs, cats, and horses. But these animals can do more than just love us back; they can help us in many ways. Animals that help others are called service animals. These animals help people do tasks that they would not be able to do alone. Service animals are not pets but working animals doing a job. Laws state that service animals can go anywhere a human can go if they are helping a human.

a two   **c** four
b three   **d** five

3 Key word: *activities*

Today, there are many activities for children to be involved in. Many of these activities are both educational and fun. They can help children develop their talents and learn new skills. Activities can also provide opportunities to learn important life skills, such as discipline and teamwork. Activities can also help kids meet other kids outside of school. Last, activities can help kids stay physically fit. There is a lot to gain from doing activities.

a two   **c** five
b three   **d** six

4 Key word: *moon*

What do you see when you look at the moon? The dark spots on the moon represent different things in different countries. In the United States, people think the shapes look like a man's face. That is how we got the expression "the man on the moon." People in other parts of the world say that these spots make a picture of a rabbit. Others see a woman reading a book. There are many images and stories of the shapes on the moon.

a two   **c** four
b three   **d** five

5 Key phrase: *average time*

You hear of people running marathons all the time—but have you ever heard of an ultramarathon? In an ultramarathon, athletes run 30 miles or more. They run through cities, over rough trails, and through forests. Some of these races are 100 miles long! An average time for a 100-mile ultramarathon is 25 hours, but the world record is 11 hours! To be an ultramarathoner, you have to really love to run!

a one   **c** three
b two   **d** four

SCANNING FOR INFORMATION

Presentation

Scanning for Information

Scanning is a way to read quickly to find key words and information. To scan a text for specific information, follow these steps:

1. Think about the information you are looking for. If you are looking for a date, scan for numbers on the page. If you are looking for a person, scan for names.

2. Only pay attention to the word you are looking for. Don't read the text for meaning.

3. Move your eyes quickly across the page until you find the information.

Practice 1

Read the question. Circle the letter of the correct answer.

Easy Family Cookbook	iv
Chapter 1: Appetizers, Snacks	1–12
Chapter 2: Beverages (hot and cold drinks).	13–17
Chapter 3: Main Dishes (beef, chicken, pork, vegetarian).	18–32
Chapter 4: Side Dishes (vegetables, fruit)	33–45
Chapter 5: Breakfast (pancakes, waffles, omelets, quiches)	46–52
Chapter 6: One-Pan Dishes (stews, soups, casseroles).	53–66
Chapter 7: Desserts (cakes, pies, cookies, candy).	67–79
Chapter 8: Appendix (cooking information, measurement aids). . .	80–88

1 In which chapter would you find a recipe for vegetable soup?
   a Chapter 1
   b Chapter 2
   c Chapter 4
   d Chapter 6

2 On what pages can you find recipes for cakes and pies?
   a Pages 1–12
   b Pages 18–32
   c Pages 67–79
   d Pages 80–88

3 A recipe for fruit salad could be found in which chapter?
   a Chapter 1
   b Chapter 4
   c Chapter 5
   d Chapter 6

4 If you need information about how many cups are in a gallon, which chapter would you need?

   a Chapter 2

   b Chapter 3

   c Chapter 7

   d Chapter 8

5 Which chapter would have recipes for hot drinks?

   a Chapter 1

   b Chapter 2

   c Chapter 4

   d Chapter 6

6 If you want a simple, one-pan meal, in which chapter would you find recipes for that?

   a Chapter 1

   b Chapter 3

   c Chapter 6

   d Chapter 7

Practice 2

Read the question. Circle the letter of the correct answer.

> **Sandwich Stop**
> 6902 Sail Road, Topsail Island 555-9375
> **Sarah's Seafood Restaurant**
> 1465 Seashore Drive, Topsail Island . . . 555-4436
> **Strikers Hotdogs**
> 8834 Sail Road, Topsail Island 555-0362
> **Surf and Turf Fine Seafood Restaurant**
> 5489 Oceanview Drive, Topsail Island . . 555-2280
> **Surf's Up Surfing School**
> 7809 Sail Road, Topsail Island 555-8740
> **Tastee Icees**
> 1309 Oceanview Drive, Topsail Island . . 555-9320
> **Tiger Tots Karate School**
> 4597 High Road, Surftown 555-6892
> **Waterway Inn**
> 8032 Oceanview Drive, Topsail Island . . 555-9469
> **Wiley's Grocery Store**
> 7922 Sail Road, Topsail Island 555-8945

1 What is the number for Tastee Icees?

  a 555-8740   **c** 555-6892

  b 555-9320   **d** 555-4436

2 Where is Waterway Inn located?

  a 7922 Sail Road, Topsail Island   **c** 6902 Sail Road, Topsail Island

  b 7809 Sail Road, Topsail Island   **d** 8032 Oceanview Drive, Topsail Island

3 Which two restaurants serve seafood?

  a Sarah's and Striker's   **c** Sandwich Stop and Striker's

  b Sarah's and Surf and Turf   **d** Sarah's and Sandwich Stop

4 Which is the only place listed outside of Topsail Island?

  a Striker's Hot Dogs   **c** Tiger Tots Karate School

  b Surf's Up Surfing School   **d** Wiley's Grocery Store

5 Where would you go if you needed to buy food to make dinner?

  a Waterway Inn   **c** Striker's Hot Dogs

  b Wiley's Grocery Store   **d** Sarah's Seafood Restaurant

6 Which restaurant's address is 6902 Sail Road?

  a Sarah's Seafood   **c** Sandwich Stop

  b Striker's Hot Dogs   **d** Surf and Turf Fine Seafood

Practice 3

Read the question. Circle the letter of the correct answer.

Ingredients	Directions:
1 cup of cut-up pineapple	1. Clean and cut all of the fruit.
½ cup of apples	Put fruit in a large bowl.
1 ½ cups of strawberries	2. Grate the ginger.
1 ½ cups of grapes	3. Mix together the lemon
1 cup of blueberries	juice, honey, and ginger.
1 teaspoon of grated ginger	4. Pour the lemon mixture over
2 tablespoons of lemon juice	the fruit.
1 ½ tablespoons of honey	5. Chill for one hour.
	6. Serve immediately.
	Makes 8 servings

1 How many cups of pineapple does the recipe call for?

  a 1

  b 1/2

  c 1 1/2

  d 2

2 How many ingredients are there?

  a 6

  b 7

  c 8

  d 9

3 How much honey does the recipe call for?

  a 1 teaspoon

  b 1 1/2 tablespoons

  c 2 tablespoons

  d 1 cup

4 Which steps are in the right order?

  a Grate the ginger; clean and cut the fruit; chill for one hour.

  b Chill for one hour; pour the lemon mixture over the fruit; grate the ginger.

  c Serve immediately; grate the ginger; mix together the lemon juice, honey, and ginger.

  d Clean and cut the fruit; grate the ginger; mix together the lemon juice, honey, and ginger.

5 How many people will this recipe serve?

  a 1

  b 2

  c 8

  d 1 1/2

Practice 4

Read the question. Circle the letter of the correct answer.

Language Arts Week 1

Week	Content	Assignment	Due Date
1	Literary elements-plot, character, setting, theme, tone	Read a fiction book and fill out the elements worksheet.	September 1
2	Fiction versus nonfiction works	Read a fiction and a nonfiction book on the same topic. Compare.	September 8
3	Imagery and symbolism in fiction	Read a fiction book. Write examples of all the imagery and symbolism in the book.	September 15
4	Point of view in fiction and nonfiction	Read a fiction and a nonfiction book. Explain how the author in both books expresses point of view.	September 22
5	Poetry	Read two different types of poems on the same topic. Compare.	September 29

1 In which week will the students study about symbolism in fiction?

  a 1   **c** 3

  b 2   **d** 4

2 In which week will they compare different types of poems?

  a 2   **c** 4

  b 3   **d** 5

3 When is the assignment on point of view due?

  a September 8   **c** September 22

  b September 15   **d** September 29

4 What will the students study in week 2?

  a Literary elements   **c** Imagery and symbolism

  b Fiction versus nonfiction works   **d** Point of view

5 In which weeks do the students have to read two books?

  a Week 1, Week 3   **c** Week 3, Week 5

  b Week 2, Week 4   **d** Week 2, Week 3

6 When is the elements worksheet due?

  a September 1   **c** September 15

  b September 8   **d** September 22

Making Inferences

MAKING INFERENCES FROM CONVERSATIONS

Presentation

Making Inferences from Dialogue

An inference is like a guess. We make inferences based on our personal experiences, the information we read, and our own knowledge about a topic.

Many times the writer doesn't give all of the information about the situation. Good readers make inferences about the missing information or what the author is trying to say. Inferences can help us understand better.

Here are some examples:

1. You read an article about an increase in crime in a certain area of the city. You make an inference from this article that it is best to stay away from that area.

2. You are scheduled to see a movie with your friend tonight. You get an email from her stating that she is sorry, but her son has soccer practice tonight. You make an inference that your friend won't be able to go to the movie tonight.

In example #1, the author doesn't tell the reader not to go to that area, but you can infer that the area would be dangerous because of the increase in crime.

In example #2, the friend didn't say she couldn't go to the movie, but you can infer that she can't go because she'll be busy with her son.

These examples show us that as readers, we need to think about what the author is saying, even though the author doesn't state it exactly. We call this "reading between the lines," or making inferences. As we read, we gather clues about the information given so that we can make inferences about what is really going on in the passage or dialogue.

Practice 1

Read the conversation and the question. Circle the letter of the best answer.

A: Has it started yet?

B: No, not yet. People are still finding their seats.

A: Good! I'll be there in a few minutes. I'm stuck in traffic. How is Mary doing?

B: She is a bit nervous about going on the stage, but we practiced her song, and she'll do great.

A: How is her throat?

B: Much better. She says it doesn't hurt anymore, and she sings fine.

A: Great. I'll see you in a bit.

B: OK. Hurry!

1 Where is person A?
   a at work
   b in the car
   c walking
   d at a store

2 Where is person B?
   a sitting in a theater
   b sitting in a car
   c sitting in a park
   d sitting at work

3 What is happening?
   a Mary is going to play a soccer game.
   b Mary is going to school.
   c Mary is going to sing a song on stage.
   d Mary is going to take a test.

4 What was wrong with Mary's throat?
   a Mary's throat was sore.
   b Mary's throat was big.
   c Mary's singing was bad.
   d Mary's throat didn't like to sing.

5 What can you infer about Mary?
   a Mary is shy to get on stage.
   b Mary doesn't sing well.
   c Mary loves to be on stage.
   d Mary hates singing.

Practice 2

Read the conversation and the question. Circle the letter of the best answer.

A: Hello?

B: Hi, Christine. It's Linda.

A: Oh, hi, Linda. What's up with you?

B: You'll never guess who I saw last night at the store.

A: Who?

B: Peter.

A: Who's that?

B: Remember the guy from the party last weekend?

A: Oh, that's right. So, how did it go?

B: My heart was pounding so fast when I first saw him. He's so cute!

A: Did you talk to him?

B: I was too nervous.

A: Oh, Linda. That's not like you!

B: Well, I guess I'm not myself since I broke up with John.

1 Who are A and B?

  a boyfriend and girlfriend

  b strangers

  c friends

  d teacher and student

2 Where are they talking?

  a They are on the phone.

  b They are at a coffee shop.

  c They are outside of class.

  d They are in a car.

3 What does Linda think about Peter?

  a She likes him.

  b She thinks he is mean.

  c She thinks he is old.

  d She thinks he is a student.

4 How long have Linda and Peter known each other?

  a 1 week

  b 1 month

  c 1 year

  d a long time

5 Did Linda speak to Peter at the store?

  a yes

  b no

6 How is Linda different after her breakup with John?

  a She is happier.

  b She is shy about talking to boys.

  c She doesn't like talking.

  d She is very outgoing.

Practice 3

Read the conversation and the question. Circle the letter of the best answer.

A: Hey, watch it!

B: I'm sorry! I didn't mean to do that.

A: Look at my dress. It's ruined. Do you know how hard it is to get coffee out of a white dress?

B: I'm really sorry. Let me ask the waiter for something to wipe it off with.

A: That's not going to work. I need to change, and I'm already late for work.

B: I'm truly sorry. Can I help pay for it?

A: Yes, that would be nice.

B: Well, here's my name and number. Please call when you have the bill.

A: OK. Thank you. I will.

B: Yes, please do. I want to help out in any way I can.

1 Who are these people?

   a strangers

   b friends

   c classmates

   d customer and waiter

2 What happened?

   a A spilled coffee on B's dress.

   b B spilled coffee on A's dress.

   c B poured coffee on A's dress.

   d A spilled coffee on her own dress.

3 Where are they?

   a They're in a coffee shop.

   b They're in class.

   c They're at work.

   d They're on the street.

4 Person B offers to pay for something. What is it?

   a her coffee

   b another cup of coffee

   c a towel

   d cleaning fees

5 How was person B feeling?

   a sick

   b happy

   c shy

   d bad

MAKING INFERENCES IN FICTION

Presentation

Making Inferences in Fiction

An inference is like a guess. We make inferences based on our personal experiences, the information we read, and our own knowledge about a topic.

Many times the writer doesn't give all of the information about the situation. Good readers make inferences about the missing information. Inferences can help us understand better.

Practice 1

Read the story and the question. Then circle the letter of the answer.

Sally was so excited. The morning after her birthday was cool and crisp. It was a perfect day for her first big ride on her new bike. It was the best birthday present ever! She loved it. Sally looked at her watch. She didn't want to keep Tyler waiting at the park.

When Sally arrived at the park, she saw Tyler hanging from the monkey bars. He jumped off and said, "Hey Sally! Are you ready for our big adventure?" Sally nodded her head, and off they raced down the path behind the park. It was bumpy at first, but Sally felt confident on her new bike.

After they rode for a while, they came upon Fox Lake. It was beautiful at this time of year. The yellow, orange, and red leaves were glowing in the sun. They hopped off and dipped their feet in the lake. At first their toes were frozen, but after a while they got used to it, and they were soon in the water up to their knees.

Sally and Tyler stayed there for a couple of hours. They were playing around and looking for wildlife. They saw some snakes, and they found a turtle. They played with it for a while and made a little house for it. After a while they let it go. Then, Sally's stomach rumbled, and they knew it was lunch time. They hopped back on their bikes and rode back to the park.

At the park, they parted ways for their houses. Sally called out, "Thanks, Tyler! That was fun!" Tyler called back, "Let's meet again tomorrow!" As Sally got home, she thought she could eat a horse! All that fresh air and biking made her hungry. She had a great time. She couldn't wait until tomorrow.

1 How old do you think Sally and Tyler are?
 a 3 years old
 b 10 years old
 c 20 years old
 d 25 years old

2 What season is it?
 a Winter
 b Summer
 c Spring
 d Fall

3 What did Sally get for her birthday?
 a a new bike
 b a new doll
 c monkey bars
 d a turtle

4 Who is Tyler?
 a Sally's brother
 b Sally's sister
 c Sally's friend
 d Sally's teacher

5 What did they make a house for?
 a their bikes
 b a snake
 c a dog
 d a turtle

6 Why did Sally's stomach rumble?
 a She was hungry.
 b She was sick.
 c The turtle bit her.
 d She was afraid to ride her bike.

7 How do Sally and Tyler feel?
 a They are happy.
 b They are shy.
 c They are anxious.
 d They are bored.

8 What will Sally and Tyler probably do tomorrow?
   a They will go to school.
   b They will stay home and play video games.
   c They will go back to the lake.
   d They will buy a turtle at the pet store.

Practice 2

Read the story and the question. Then circle the letter of the answer.

The Smith family were on their way back from their family vacation. They had spent two wonderful weeks camping in the mountains. The drive back to their house was long. It was late, and Mr. Smith and the children, Tommy and Tina, were all asleep in the back seats. Mrs. Smith was at the wheel.

After a while, Mrs. Smith got a little thirsty. She stopped at a restaurant. Everyone was still asleep, so she slipped quietly out of the car and went inside the restaurant. Meanwhile, Mr. Smith woke up and realized he had to go to the bathroom. He also slipped out of the car and went inside.

A few minutes later, Mrs. Smith got back in the car and drove off. She felt much better and was ready to drive some more. She was going to wake up Mr. Smith when she got tired, but for now she felt good, and she felt that she could finish the drive home. She decided she would let Mr. Smith sleep.

A few hours later, they arrived back home. The kids were still asleep in the car, so she carefully carried them inside the house. When she went to unpack the car, she didn't see her husband. She thought he had gone inside the house. She unpacked the bags and went to bed. A few minutes later, the telephone rang. It was Mr. Smith, and he didn't sound happy!

1 Where are they in the beginning of the story?
   a in a car
   b in the mountains
   c at home
   d at a restaurant

2 Who was driving?
   a Mr. Smith
   b Mrs. Smith
   c Tommy
   d Tina

3 Why was everyone asleep in the car?

    a They were all sick of driving.

    b They were hurt from hiking in the mountains.

    c They were pretending to be asleep.

    d They were tired from their vacation.

4 Why did Mrs. Smith stop at a restaurant?

    a She was sleeping.

    b She was bored.

    c She needed a drink.

    d She needed some food.

5 Why did Mrs. Smith drive off without Mr. Smith?

    a She was mad at him.

    b She didn't know he wasn't in the car.

    c She forgot he was inside the restaurant.

    d He told her to leave him behind.

6 Where do you think Mr. Smith was in the end?

    a He was in the mountains.

    b He was in the car.

    c He was at the restaurant.

    d He was walking home.

7 At the end of the story, how was Mr. Smith feeling?

    a tired

    b sleepy

    c sick

    d mad

8 At the end of the story, how was Mrs. Smith feeling?

    a sleepy

    b sick

    c confused

    d mad

Practice 3

Read the story and the question. Then circle the letter of the answer.

Once upon a time there was a farmer who lived with his dog, Max, and other animals. The other animals didn't like Max very much. He was greedy and didn't leave them much food. Also, he didn't help the animals with their jobs. He liked to laze around in the sun doing nothing. Whenever the other animals asked him to help, he would growl at them. So they stopped asking him.

One morning, Max saw a big piece of meat on the table. He knew that he had to act fast before the farmer came in from outside. He took it and ran out the door and didn't stop until he reached a river nearby.

He wanted to run a little farther from home, so he needed to cross the river. He saw a bridge that went to the other side of the river. As he was crossing the bridge, he looked in the water and saw another dog with a bigger piece of meat than his!

Max wanted that piece of meat, too. He thought to himself, "I can scare that dog into giving me his piece of meat, and then I'll have two!" So, just as he opened his mouth to growl, his piece of meat fell into the river and sank to the bottom, and the other dog disappeared. Distraught by having lost two pieces of meat, Max walked home with his head hung low. In his pursuit for two pieces of meat, he ended up with none.

1 Where does this story take place?

a in a city

b on a farm

c in a house

d at a zoo

2 Why don't the other animals like Max?

a He steals their food and doesn't do any work.

b He is too big.

c He is a dog.

d The farmer likes him best.

3 Why don't the animals tell the farmer about Max?

a They don't want to hurt Max's feelings.

b They don't want to make the farmer mad.

c They are afraid of Max.

d They are afraid of the farmer.

4 What is Max's personality?

a He is hard-working.

b He is mean.

c He is kind.

d He is helpful.

5 Why did he want to get farther from home after he took the piece of meat?

a He didn't want the farmer to catch him.

b He didn't want the other animals to take the meat.

c He wanted to exercise.

d He wanted to take a run in the forest.

6 What was in the river?

    a another dog with a piece of meat

    b a farm animal tricking the dog

    c Max's reflection

    d a fish

7 What happened when Max growled at the dog in the water?

    a The meat fell out of his mouth, and it sank in the river.

    b The other dog got the meat.

    c He ate the meat.

    d He got the other piece of meat, too.

8 How did Max feel in the end?

    a sleepy

    b sick

    c confused

    d sad

THINKING IN ENGLISH

> **Presentation**
>
> **Thinking in English**
>
> Good readers think about what they are reading and about what comes next. They get an idea about what words will come next before they even see them. So, when they see the words, they can look at them quickly and move on to the next sentence. Thinking ahead in English can help us become better, faster readers.
>
> Here is an example:
>
> > It was a hot, summer day. Sam had been playing outside with his friends all morning. His mother saw that they all looked quite hot and thirsty. She filled a big pitcher with _____ from the faucet in the kitchen and brought it to them.
>
> From the first sentence, we know that it is hot and it is summer. We also learn that Sam and his friends had been playing outside. The mother sees that they all look hot and thirsty. What do you usually do when you are hot and thirsty? You drink some sort of liquid. Then, we know that the liquid is coming from a faucet in the kitchen.
>
> All of these clues tell us the missing word must be *water*.
>
> If you can think ahead while you are reading, you will become faster and better at understanding what you read.

Practice 1

Circle the letter of the correct word to complete each sentence.

1 Last Saturday we went to the pool. Everyone was swimming except for Tommy. He thought that the water was too _____ .

a cold   **c** crowded
b wet   **d** warm

2 Children should not play too many video games. They are not good for their minds. Children should _____ outside more often. Fresh air is good for them.

a play   **c** sleep
b read   **d** eat

3 Libraries are an important part of our community. Reading is an important skill. Allowing people to check out _____ free of charge encourages people to read more.

a books   **c** videos
b music   **d** food

4 Many years ago, people didn't have heat in their houses. In the cold months, people had to build fires in their _____ .

a walls   **c** houses
b fireplaces   **d** floor

5 People get their _____ from many sources now. Television news programs, newspapers, and the Internet are popular ways to find out what is going on in the world.

a music   **c** entertainment
b stores   **d** news

6 If you are outside in a thunderstorm, it is important that you find _____ in a building or a car. Lightning can be very dangerous.

a shelter   **c** wood
b food   **d** light

7 Juan just learned how to ride a motorcycle. He borrowed his brother's motorcycle to practice. He passed the test yesterday, so now that he got his _____ , he is going to buy his own.

a license   **c** practice
b motorcycle   **d** car

8 Tom really likes to play sports. He plays a _____ sport every day of the week. His favorite sports are basketball, soccer, and baseball.

a difficult   **c** fun
b different   **d** ball

Practice 2

Circle the letter of the correct word to complete each sentence.

1 My brother works at a donut shop. He has to be there very early in the morning to help make the donuts. He sometimes _____ before we are even out of bed!
 a gets home
 b goes to sleep
 c drinks a coffee
 d has a donut

2 I used to go dancing _____ , but now I only go once a month. Since I started school, I don't have any time to go during the week.
 a all the time
 b around my house
 c in my class
 d once a year

3 Every Sunday my dog, Sierra, and I go for a drive in the country. Sierra loves to _____ . She sticks her head out the window to feel the fresh air on her face.
 a take walks
 b fall asleep
 c ride in a car
 d listen to music

4 That roller coaster was amazing! Let's _____ !
 a eat some food
 b do it again
 c read a book
 d go to school now

5 Joe studied all last week. He went to the library every day. He talked with his professors, and he met with his classmates. I am really proud of him. I hope he _____ .
 a drops out of school
 b passes the test
 c plays tennis
 d rides his bike

6 Sam _____ last week. He is still in the hospital, but he is coming home tomorrow.
 a played soccer
 b studied hard
 c went on vacation
 d was in an accident

7 Yoko is going to visit her parents in Japan next week. She is going to
_____ for 10 days. She asked me to take notes for her.

   a miss school

   b pack her bag

   c listen in class

   d do homework

8 Tomorrow is Jenny's birthday. Let's meet after work so we can all
_____ . She really likes that new restaurant downtown.

   a take her out

   b study with her

   c take her home

   d go to the park

Recognizing Patterns

LISTING PATTERN

Presentation

Listing Pattern

Many texts list examples, details, and facts. The author uses certain signal words to tell the reader about the list. Some of these signal words include:

- Many
- Several

- A lot of
- Lots of

- Some
- A few

After the author tells the reader about the list, the supporting sentences state the things on the list. These sentences usually start with signal words, such as:

- First, Second, Third…
- One
- Other
- Another

- In addition
- Last
- Finally
- And

- Also
- Too
- Yet another
- For example

Practice 1

Read the paragraph. Underline all the listing signal words.

1 There are many types of traditional clothing around the world. One type is the kilt in Scotland. A kilt is a plaid skirt worn by men. Another kind of clothing is the sari in India. This consists of long, colorful cloth and is worn by women. The kimono, worn in Japan, is yet another type of traditional clothing. Kimonos are usually made out of silk and are tightly wrapped around a woman's body. The last example is the headdress of the American Indian. This is usually worn by the men in a tribe. It is made out of leather, and it has colorful feathers hanging down the back. These are just a few examples of different traditional clothing around the world.

2 If you are looking for a sport that is done both by individuals but also as a team, then track and field is the sport for you. There are a lot of events within the sport of track and field. Most of these events are done individually, but together the individuals earn points for their team. One event is the 50-yard dash. In this event, the athletes sprint to the finish line. If running fast is not for you, another event is the mile run. Athletes run a mile to the finish line. Other events don't involve running. For example, the long jump, the high jump, and the shot put are all events where you don't have to run. So, as you can see, there are many events within the sport of track and field. There is something for everyone.

3 Many people nowadays get their news from the Internet. There are several reasons for this. First, it is more convenient. Most households have computers or smartphones with Internet capabilities. It is more convenient to look on your computer as you are working than to find a newspaper. Also, the Internet is cheaper. Again, as most people already have Internet access at work or at home, having to buy a newspaper subscription is an added cost. Last, the Internet is more current. The news sites are able to update people with the most up-to-date information, whereas a newspaper has to wait until the next printing to get the news out. For these reasons, the Internet is taking over as the primary way people get their news.

4   Before we had coins and paper for currency, people used many things for money. One type of popular currency was grains, such as rice and barley. This is understandable, since rice and barley can be eaten, and food is necessary for survival. Other types of currency were animals, such as fish and cows. Again, this is understandable, since these animals can be used for food or milk. In addition to these things needed for survival, there were other more frivolous currencies, such as beads and belts. These were used for decoration, not survival, but nonetheless they were used as money. One final example of money was bat droppings, or guano. Since bat droppings are rich in nutrients, it helps plants and crops grow. Bat guano is still sold today, but it is not used as money anymore.

Practice 2

Part 1

Read the paragraph. Write the number of the sentences in the correct box. Write the number of the sentence with the main idea that states a list under A and the sentences that list the examples under B.

In summer, thunderstorms can brew up at a moment's notice. There are several things you can do if you find yourself outside in a thunderstorm. First, seek shelter either in a car or in a building. Lightning is attracted to metal, so do not seek shelter in a metal building. If you are in a car, do not touch anything metal. Second, do not swim or go boating. If you are on a boat, find shelter on land as soon as possible. These tips can help save your life!

1   First, seek shelter either in a car or in a building.
2   There are several things you can do if you find yourself outside in a thunderstorm.
3   Second, do not swim or go boating.

A: Main idea sentence with signal word stating list	B: Supporting detail sentences with signal words that list examples

Part 2

Read the paragraph. Write the number of the sentences in the correct box as in Part 1.

Once you find shelter inside, here are some tips to remember. One, don't use the telephone or any electrical appliance, such as a hair dryer or radio. Also, don't stand or sit in front of the television. Lightning can strike a TV even when it is turned off. In addition, be sure to unplug it along with your computer. If lightning strikes an appliance, it will be destroyed.

1 In addition, be sure to unplug it along with your computer.

2 Once you find shelter inside, here are some tips to remember.

3 One, don't use the telephone or any electrical appliance, such as a hair dryer or radio.

4 Also, don't stand or sit in front of the television.

A: Main idea sentence with signal word stating list	B: Supporting detail sentences with signal words that list examples

Part 3

Read the paragraph. Write the number of the sentences in the correct box, as in Part 1.

If you can't find indoor shelter, then here are a few tips. First, squat low to the ground and place your head between your knees. Lightning will strike the tallest object around, so try to make yourself very short. Also, do not sit or stand under a tree or a pole. Again, lightning will be attracted to tall objects. Finally, wait until the storm has completely passed to come out. Lightning can travel and strike from many miles away. It is important to remember these things. Lightning storms can be very dangerous.

1　Also, do not sit or stand under a tree or pole.

2　First, squat low to the ground and place your head between your knees.

3　If you can't find indoor shelter, then here are a few tips.

4　Finally, wait until the storm has completely passed to come out.

A: Main idea sentence with signal word stating list	B: Supporting detail sentences with signal words that list examples

SEQUENCE PATTERN

Presentation

Sequence Pattern

Many texts list a sequence of things that happen in order. Some examples can be a sequence of events, such as events in a person's life, dates in history, etc.

Other sequences relate to steps in a process, such as instructions on how to do something or directions for going somewhere.

The author uses certain signal words to tell the reader that the paragraph will include a sequence. Some of these signal words include:

* History
* Life
* How

* Make
* Do
* Learn

* The way to
* Process
* Steps

After the author tells the reader about the sequence, the supporting sentences state steps or stages of a person's life. These sentences usually start with signal words such as:

* First, Second, Third…
* Before
* Soon
* While
* Now
* At last
* Finally
* When
* At first

* Then
* Now
* Next
* Last
* After
* During
* For a year
* In a month
* The same day

* At this time
* Today
* Last week
* Many years
* Later
* By the 1980s
* Every
* Each

Or the author may just give a date, a time, or the age of a person to signify the place it takes in the sequence.

Practice 1

Read the paragraph. Underline all the sequence signal words.

1   Gold! You could find gold anywhere, some people said of the Gold Rush. In 1849, the Gold Rush in California began. Soon, people flocked to the hills of California in hopes of striking it rich. A few years later, a young man named Levi Strauss also came to California. When he arrived, he changed his focus from gold to supplies. He knew that everyone needed basic supplies. So, at last he decided to make his fortune by selling items to the gold miners instead of searching for gold.

2   After Levi made his decision to sell supplies, he stocked up on dry goods like thread, needles, scissors, combs, kettles, and shoes. When miners arrived in California, they only owned the shirts on their backs. So as soon as they got there, they needed to buy supplies, and Levi was the man to sell it to them!

3 The first thing that Levi noticed was the miners' pants. They wore ragged pants made of cheap material that wasn't very durable. Miners often worked on their hands and knees digging for gold, and their poorly made pants couldn't take the roughness of the land. At that time, Levi got an idea to make stronger pants.

4 When Levi was getting ready to go to California, he packed some strong canvas material. One day, he got an idea that this canvas would be perfect to make stronger pants. The next day, he took the canvas to a tailor to help him make some pants. These first pairs of pants, called jeans, sold very well. As soon as he sold one pair, he got a lot of orders to make more.

5 Levi's jeans were selling like hotcakes, so in 1856, he opened up a bigger shop. Soon, he put up a big sign that read, "Levi Strauss & Co." After that, Levi Strauss & Co. continued to grow through the years. Every few years, he had to move to a bigger building. Each time he moved, he hired more employees. Levi's business was booming!

6 After a few years, Levi couldn't get enough of the tan canvas to keep up with the orders. Soon he found a different fabric that was just as sturdy. That fabric was denim, which is the same material most jeans are made out of today. The big difference between the denim and the canvas was the color. The denim was blue. Soon after, these popular pants became known as "blue jeans," and they are just as popular today as they were during the Gold Rush days.

Practice 2

Read the paragraph. Write the number of the sentences in the correct box on p. 71. Write the number of the sentence with the main idea that states a list under A and the sentences that list the examples under B.

There are many types of jeans today. It doesn't matter which kind you wear, since they are all made from the same material and in the same way. In the mid-1800s, Levi Strauss made the first pair of blue jeans. The process he used back then is the same we use today.

First, you start with a pattern. Draw each piece of the jeans (pockets, front part of leg, back part of leg, etc.) on heavy cardboard. Each pair of jeans is made out of about ten different pieces.

Next, buy the fabric and other supplies, such as thread and buttons. You can get these at any fabric store. There are many different colors of denim today. The traditional dark blue is always popular, but nowadays you can also find light blue, white, and even other colors, such as green and pink.

After you have bought the fabric, roll it out on a large table. Next, put the cardboard patterns on top of the fabric and, using a heavy-duty scissors or machine, cut the pieces out.

After the fabric is cut, the pieces are sewn together. Sewing the jeans together is the biggest part of the job. This is done in several simple steps. First, you make the belt loops. Then, you attach the pockets. After that, you stitch up the pant legs and put on a waistband. Next, you attach the buttons. They can be any type of button. Finally, add a zipper, and you are done!

1 First, you make the belt loops.
2 Next, buy the fabric and other supplies, such as thread and buttons.
3 This is done in several simple steps.
4 After the fabric is cut, the pieces are sewn together.
5 The process he used back then is the same we use today.
6 Next, you attach the buttons.
7 After that, you stitch up the pant legs and put on a waistband.
8 Finally, add a zipper, and you are done!
9 After you have bought the fabric, roll it out on a large table.
10 Then you attach the pockets.
11 Next, put the cardboard patterns on top of the fabric and, using a heavy-duty scissors or machine, cut the pieces out.
12 First, you start with a pattern.

A: Main idea sentence with signal word stating a sequence	B: Supporting detail sentences with signal words that list steps

COMPARISON PATTERN

Comparison Pattern

Many texts compare two things, people, or ideas. The author tells us how they are similar, different, or both.

The author uses certain signal words to tell the reader that the paragraph will include a comparison. Some of these signal words include:

- The two things, people, or ideas that will be compared
- Any of the words in the list below

After the author tells the reader about the comparison, the supporting sentences tell about the ways the two things or people are similar or different. These sentences usually have signal words.

For sentences that show how the two things are the same:

- Alike
- Like
- Similar
- Same
- Also
- Both
- Too

For sentences that show how the two things are different:

- Different
- Differ
- Unlike
- But
- However
- While
- On the other hand
- Whereas

For sentences that show a comparison between the two things:

- More than
- Less than
- Bigger
- Smaller
- More beautiful

Practice 1

Read each paragraph. Underline all the comparison signal words, including words that show similarities and words that show differences.

1 I love to eat! I have many favorite foods, but two of my favorite cuisines are very different from each other: German and Mexican. For the main meal, Germans like meat, and so with every meal there is a big piece of meat on the plate. Mexicans like meat, too, but it is usually cut up or shredded and in a corn or flour tortilla. As for side dishes, Germans cook with a lot of noodles and potatoes. Mexicans, however, have rice and beans as sides to their main dishes. Spice is another way they are very different. Except for mustard, German food is rarely hot and spicy. They may use herbs in their food, such as parsley, thyme, and black pepper, but nothing that has a strong flavor. Mexicans, on the other hand, love hot and spicy food. They use chili peppers in every meal to heat up the flavor. Foods from Germany and Mexico are very different, but I like them both.

2 After college, I lived in Japan for five years. It was a wonderful time in my life. I learned a lot about the Japanese people and culture. There are many things that are different culturally between Japan and the United States. We differ in the way we greet one another. In Japan, people bow to each other. There is no physical contact. However, in the U.S., a handshake or a hug is the usual way to greet one another. Another difference is that Japanese people take off their shoes in their homes. In the U.S., people keep their shoes on in the house. Another way we are unlike one another in the home is that they often sit on the ground to eat at low tables, but in the U.S., we sit on chairs at higher tables. I thought these cultural differences were quite interesting. I really enjoyed my time in Japan.

3 Often times it may seem that men and women are from different planets. We are obviously both humans, but the way in which we communicate is so very different. One way men and women differ is the number of times they say sorry. Women apologize a lot more than men do. Another point is how much each speaks. Women talk often. They connect with their female friends by talking, while men don't talk very much but connect with their male friends by doing things together. We are also unlike each other when it comes to fixing things. Women tend to find a professional to fix a broken item, whereas men try to fix it themselves. Despite our differences, men and women work well together as a team in many ways. We complement our differences.

4 When you have vacation, where do you like to go? Would you rather go to the beach or the mountains? Both can be great vacation spots. In many ways, the beach and the mountains are alike. We may wonder how the beach and the mountains could be similar. Here are a few ways. Both vacation spots offer a relaxing view. Looking out at the ocean or across a mountain range brings peace and tranquillity to many people. If you like to take walks and be in the fresh air, then both the beach and the mountains can offer that, too. Another similarity is the opportunities for being active. In both places you can get a lot of exercise, either by swimming or playing volleyball on the beach or hiking and biking in the mountains. The next time you have some vacation time, it may be difficult to decide between these two great places.

Practice 2

Read the paragraph. Write the number of the sentences in the correct box on p. 76:

- Write the number of the sentence with the main idea that tells us there will be a comparison under category A.
- Write the number of the sentences that give examples of similarity under category B.
- Write the number of the sentences that give examples of differences under category C.
- Write the number of the sentences that give examples of comparison under category D.

You see turtles in lakes and you see turtles in the ocean. How are they different from one another? The turtles that live in lakes are called land turtles, and the ones that live in the ocean are called sea turtles. There are many differences between these two types of turtles. First, land turtles live mostly on land, while sea turtles live almost entirely in the water. The only time they come on land is to lay eggs in the sand.

Because sea turtles live underwater, their body differs from land turtles. Sea turtles have flippers. These help the sea turtle to swim. However, land turtles have four legs. These legs help the land turtle walk on land. Another difference is their head. Sea turtles cannot pull their head or legs in for protection. On the other hand, a land turtle can pull its head and legs inside its shell to protect itself from predators, such as raccoons and snakes.

Both turtles are good swimmers. However, the sea turtle is a better swimmer than the land turtle. A sea turtle can also hold its breath longer than a land turtle. Some sea turtles can stay underwater up to five hours before coming up for air! They are both classified as reptiles since they have a bony back with a hard shell. The next time you come across a turtle, see if you can notice the different features mentioned in this article. They are both beautiful creatures that have lived on this planet a long time!

1 They are both classified as reptiles since they have a bony back with a hard shell.

2 However, land turtles have four legs.

3 The turtles that live in lakes are called land turtles, and the ones that live in the ocean are called sea turtles.

4 They are both beautiful creatures that have lived on this planet a long time!

5 Another difference is their head.

6 On the other hand, a land turtle can pull its head and legs inside its shell to protect itself from predators, such as raccoons and snakes.

7 There are many differences between these two types of turtles.

8 Because sea turtles live underwater, their body differs from land turtles.

9 Both turtles are good swimmers.

10 A sea turtle can also hold its breath longer than a land turtle.

11 However, the sea turtle is a better swimmer than the land turtle.

A: Main idea sentence with signal words stating a comparison	B: Supporting detail sentences with signal words that show similarities
C: Supporting detail sentences with signal words that show differences	D: Supporting detail sentences with signal words that show comparisons

Identifying Patterns

Presentation

Identifying the Correct Pattern

Here is a summary of the three different kinds of patterns you learned:

The listing pattern: This type of paragraph lists reasons, details, examples, or ideas.

The sequence pattern: This type of paragraph tells about events or steps in a certain order.

The comparison pattern: This type of paragraph compares two things or people by explaining their similarities or differences.

Practice 1

Read each paragraph. Which kind of pattern does it have? Is it a listing pattern, a sequence pattern, or a comparison pattern? Circle the letter of the correct answer.

1 A vegetarian is someone who does not eat meat. There are many reasons people become vegetarians. Some people simply do not like the taste of meat. Others believe it is cruel to eat meat from an animal. Then, there are some people whose religion does not allow them to eat meat. Last, there are some people who think it is unhealthy to eat meat. Vegetarians eat a lot of vegetables, fruits, beans, and soy products, such as tofu. Whatever the reason, the number of vegetarians is increasing all over the world.

   a listing pattern

   b sequence pattern

   c comparison pattern

2 One day a shop owner saw a man steal some food from his store. Before the man went out of the store, the owner caught him. The owner asked him why he stole the food. The man said that he needed it to feed his family. He said he lost his job, and now he has no money. As soon as the owner heard the story, he let him go with the food. Before the man left though, the owner told him to come back tomorrow. The next day the man came back, and the owner gave him a job. After he got the job, the man never stole again.

   a listing pattern

   b sequence pattern

   c comparison pattern

3 To read a paper book or to read an e-reader: that is the question. Electronic books, or e-readers, are becoming very popular. Even though both paper books and e-readers are ways to read, there are many differences between the two types of books. In a paper book, you can see how much further you have to read. You can tell by the thickness of the book how many pages you have left to read. Some people like to see their progress when reading. However, with an e-reader you don't have that visual. Another way they differ is that in a paper book, you can flip back and forth between

pages easily and quickly. If you want to go back to a different page, you can quickly access that page. On the other hand, with an e-reader, you have to go back one page at a time to find what you're looking for. One of the advantages of an e-reader is that it has its own light. If you like to read in bed, you don't need another light to read, while with a paper book, you need a light to see what you're reading. There are advantages to both kinds of books. The important thing is that you're reading!

a listing pattern
b sequence pattern
c comparison pattern

4 If you have an animal, then you know that finding a good veterinarian is important. A veterinarian is a doctor who specializes in the treatment of animals. There are three types of veterinarians. There are some who take care of large animals, such as horses, cows, and sheep. Other veterinarians take care of small animals, such as cats and dogs. The last type of veterinarian takes care of exotic animals, such as snakes, lizards, and zoo animals. Each type of veterinarian is important for the well-being of all types of animals.

a listing pattern
b sequence pattern
c comparison pattern

Practice 2

Read each paragraph. Which kind of pattern does it have? Is it a listing pattern, a sequence pattern, or a comparison pattern? Circle the letter of the correct answer.

1 Every weekend my friends and I go out for dinner. We have many good restaurants in our city. For example, there is a great Chinese restaurant downtown. I really like the dumplings there. In addition to the Chinese restaurant, there is a little noodle shop near my house. The noodles there are really good, and it's always cheap and fast food. Also, there is a nice French restaurant. It's a little expensive, but it is fun to go there for special occasions. Another favorite restaurant is the Brazilian Steak House. They have many kinds of meat on their menu. This weekend we are going there. I can't wait!

a listing pattern
b sequence pattern
c comparison pattern

2 Mahatma Gandhi was one of the world's greatest leaders, and he had an amazing life. He was born in 1869 in Porbandar, India. At the age of 13, Gandhi got married to a girl the same age. During their marriage they had four children. In 1888, Gandhi went to London to study law, and he returned to India in 1891 to become a lawyer. Two years later, he went to South Africa to work. After working 13 years in South Africa, he saw how Indians were discriminated against in that country. He started a nonviolent protest against the government. He wanted everyone to be treated equally. In 1913, he was arrested and jailed after leading 2,500 Indians in a nonviolent demonstration in South Africa. After his time in jail, he went back to his native country and began to work for

the people of India. During this time, he led many peaceful demonstrations against the government, asking for equal treatment of all the people in India. One part of his demonstrations was fasting. Fasting is when you don't eat anything. Gandhi fasted to make a political point. He became very famous and helped improve the lives of the poorest people in India. Because of this, some people didn't like him, and in 1948 Gandhi was killed on his way to evening prayers by a Hindu fanatic.

a listing pattern

b sequence pattern

c comparison pattern

3 There are many important people who serve our community, but two of the most important are fire fighters and police officers. Even though these two occupations have their differences, the fundamentals of their jobs are the same. They both save people. Firefighters save people from burning buildings, and police officers save people from dangerous situations. Another way they are alike is the fact that they both put their lives in danger to help others. Rushing into a burning building is the last thing most people would want to do, but for fire fighters, it's a part of their job. And most people would run the other way from an armed criminal, but police officers run toward the danger in order to keep us all safe. Both of these people deserve our gratitude and appreciation for everything they do for our community.

a listing pattern

b sequence pattern

c comparison pattern

4 My brother's new car has a lot of nice features. For example, it has a sun roof. He can open up the top of the car and see the sky. Another good feature is the leather seats. Leather is so comfortable. Also, the seats have a heater! So, in the winter time, the seats are warm. Other good parts about his car are the color, the speed, and the radio. I like it a lot. I want one, too!

a listing pattern

b sequence pattern

c comparison pattern

Comprehension Skills Practice Test

Part 1   Previewing

Preview the cover of the book. Answer the question.

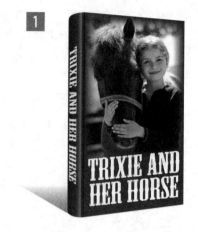

1 What type of book is this?

  a nonfiction about how to care for horses

  b fictional story about a magic horse in a magical world

  c fictional story about a girl and her horse

  d nonfiction about types of horses

2 Who is this book for?

  a children

  b teachers

  c doctors

  d parents

3 What type of book is this?

  a a story about a teacher

  b a book to help you learn to read faster

  c a story about a student who reads fast

  d a book to help you learn how to read

4 What kind of book is this?

  a nonfiction about how fairy tales relate to the world

  b a fictional story about the world

  c nonfiction about how the world was formed

  d a collection of fictional stories from different countries

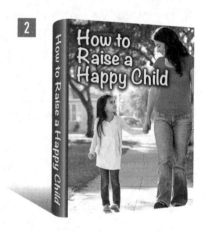

Part 2 Predicting

Look at the picture and read the title. What ideas will be in the text? Write the number of each description in the correct box.

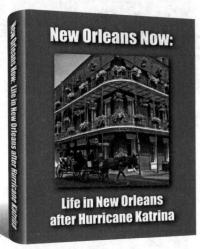

1 what to put in a hurricane survival kit

2 memorials and statues built to remember the people who died in Katrina

3 how the city rebuilt homes, schools, and roads

4 the celebration of Mardi Gras in New Orleans

5 how the storm changed the city

6 places to go when visiting New Orleans

7 how hurricanes are formed

Ideas in the book	Ideas not in the book

Tax-Free Weekend: Shopping + No Taxes = Big Savings

1 a list of items that you don't have to pay taxes on

2 how to make money

3 the dates of the weekend

4 activities to do on the weekend

5 how to get a weekend job

6 how to get free items this weekend

7 the amount of tax

8 information about the tax-free program

Ideas in the article	Ideas not in the article

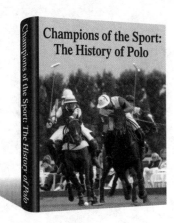

1 how polo has changed over the years

2 how horseback polo is different from water polo

3 famous polo players of the past

4 how to buy tickets to see a polo match

5 the original rules of polo

6 how polo began

7 a schedule of upcoming polo matches

8 how to train to be a polo player

Ideas in the book	Ideas not in the book

Part 3   Previewing and Predicting

Preview the Table of Contents and circle the letter of the correct answer.

1 If you want to take a relaxing vacation in a beautiful resort, which chapter should you read?

   a Chapter 1

   b Chapter 3

   c Chapter 5

   d Chapter 6

2 If you want to help someone while you are on vacation, which chapter should you read?

   a Chapter 2

   b Chapter 3

   c Chapter 4

   d Chapter 7

3 If you want to see the places close to your home while on vacation, which chapter should you read?

   a Chapter 1

   b Chapter 3

   c Chapter 6

   d Chapter 5

4 If you want some adventure on your vacation, which chapter should you read?

   a Chapter 2

   b Chapter 3

   c Chapter 6

   d Chapter 7

5 If you want to go someplace unusual and out of the ordinary, which chapter should you read?

   a Chapter 1

   b Chapter 2

   c Chapter 5

   d Chapter 7

6 If you want to stay at someone else's house while they stay at yours, which chapter should you read?

   a Chapter 1

   b Chapter 4

   c Chapter 5

   d Chapter 6

Part 4   Identifying Topics, Main Ideas, and Details

Read the passage. Is it a paragraph? Circle the letter of your answer.

1 There are many kinds of nuts in the world. Some are large like the Brazil nut and the cashew, but the coconut is the largest nut. Some are small like the peanut or the pine nut. All nuts have a lot of protein, but each individual nut provides different health benefits. They also vary significantly in their fat content and number of calories.

Doctors say that even though nuts can be high in fat, they are a healthy snack. Enjoy nuts whenever you can. They are a great addition to your diet.

a a paragraph

b not a paragraph

2 Sacagawea, a famous Native American, was an important part of American history. There are many Native American tribes. Lewis and Clark were mapmakers, and Sacagawea helped them make the map of the western part of North America. Montana is a state within the western part of the United States. It is mostly uninhabited. Montana has the largest number of elk in the United States.

a a paragraph

b not a paragraph

Part 5 Identifying Topics, Main Ideas, and Details

Read the passage. Write the number of the sentences in the correct box.

There are many kinds of nuts in the world. Some are large like the Brazil nut and the cashew, but the coconut is the largest nut. Some are small like the peanut or the pine nut. All nuts have a lot of protein, but each individual nut provides different health benefits. They also vary significantly in their fat content and number of calories. Doctors say that even though nuts can be high in fat, they are a healthy snack. Enjoy nuts whenever you can. They are a great addition to your diet.

1 There are many kinds of nuts in the world.

2 Enjoy nuts whenever you can. They are a great addition to your diet.

3 They also vary significantly in their fat content and number of calories.

4 Doctors say that even though nuts can be high in fat, they are a healthy snack.

5 All nuts have a lot of protein, but each individual nut provides different health benefits.

6 Some are large like the Brazil nut and the cashew, but the coconut is the largest nut.

7 Some are small like the peanut or the pine nut.

Topic Sentence	Body Sentences	Concluding Sentence

Part 6   Identifying the Topic of a Paragraph

Read the sentences. Circle the letter of the correct answer.

1   There is a popular saying about diamonds: "Diamonds are a girl's best friend." Diamonds are one of the most valuable gems in the world and therefore are the most expensive. They have many special qualities. They are the hardest gems on Earth, and they sparkle in the light like no other gem. Diamonds are traditionally used in wedding rings and therefore are known as the gem of love.

The topic of the paragraph is

   a   best friends.
   b   gems.
   c   diamonds.
   d   qualities.

2   One of the most famous monuments around the world is the Taj Mahal. It was created by the emperor Shah Jahan in the mid-17th century for his favorite wife. More than 20,000 people and 1,000 elephants worked for over twenty years to make the Taj Mahal. In 2007, it was named as one of the Seven Wonders of the World. More than four million tourists visit the Taj Mahal every year. It is truly a marvelous monument.

The topic of the paragraph is

   a   famous monuments.
   b   the Taj Mahal.
   c   the Seven Wonders of the World.
   d   Shah Jahan.

Part 7   Identifying the Main Idea

Read the essay. Underline the sentence that gives you the main idea.

1   There are many tropical paradises around the world. One of the most beautiful places to visit is Hawaii. Hawaii is a group of islands in the Pacific Ocean. There are four main islands that tourists typically go to. They are Oahu, Maui, Kauai, and Hawaii Island, which is often referred to as "the big island." Each one is unique and has something special to offer.

2   Although all of the islands are beautiful, there is one that many people think is the most beautiful. Kauai is known for its dramatic and natural beauty. It is often a place for people looking for a romantic vacation, as it is a bit more secluded than the other islands. The beaches of the Coconut Coast and the Waimea Canyon are two highlights of Kauai. Even though this canyon isn't as big as the Grand Canyon in Arizona, it is nicknamed "the Grand Canyon of the Pacific."

3   Many of the Hawaii islands have natural and cultural wonders, but there is one that has a vibrant mix of nature and art. Oahu is the state capital and home to the majority of Hawaii's population. There are many things to see on Oahu. The monuments and museums of Pearl Harbor are visited by thousands of tourists each year. These memorials tell of the terrible day in U.S. history. Many tourists looking for adventure or at least to witness adventurous spirits go to the North Shore to see the professional surfers take on the big waves.

4   The second-largest island in the chain is home to what most believe are the most beautiful beaches in the world. Maui has many stunning beaches that are every color, including white, red, and black. The waters off of Maui are also a great place to whale watch in the winter time. Lahaina is a town that is rich with history and has lots of restaurants and shops. If you are looking for a scenic drive, the road to Hana is one of the most famous roads in the entire world. Its windy drive takes you through beautiful tropical forests and cute little towns.

5   One of the islands has one of the world's most active volcanoes, Kilauea. Hawaii, also known as the Big Island, is the largest of all the islands. It has every type of climate from sandy beaches to snow-capped mountains. You can see everything from waterfalls and rainforests to botanical gardens. Kona is a popular city on the island, and it is known for calm and clear water. If you like coffee, there are many coffee plantations near Kona. This rich-tasting coffee, simply known as Kona coffee, is famous around the world.

6   If you want a little bit of everything, it is easy to travel from one island to the next, so you don't have to choose just one to visit. There are daily flights to and from the islands. Or if you would rather travel by sea, there are ferry boats that can transport you to the various islands. With all their natural beauty and history, there is something for everyone on the Hawaiian islands.

Part 8   Supporting Details

Read the sentences. Write the number of the sentences in the correct box.

1 Yoga is a great sport.
2 You can do it inside your house or outside.
3 Yoga can be done anywhere.
4 It is good for your body and mind.
5 The beach is a wonderful place to do yoga.

Main Idea	Supporting Details

1 Every country has some sort of tea.
2 Although it is not unhealthy, tea has a lot of caffeine.
3 Tea is one of the oldest drinks in history.
4 Historically, it was a valuable item used for money and trading purposes.

Main Idea	Supporting Details

Part 9   Scanning for Information

First, read the question. Then scan the information. Circle the letter of the correct answer.

Family Fitness Gym
Class Descriptions and Schedules

Class	Description	Schedule
Early Bird	Be the early bird and get up and get moving. This early morning class is for adults only.	Monday–Friday, 5:00 A.M.
All in One	Workout consists of running, biking, and swimming. Ages 15 and up.	Mondays: 9:00 A.M., 4:30 P.M. Wednesdays: 9:00 A.M. Fridays: 9:00 A.M., 4:30 P.M. Saturdays: 7:00 A.M.
Stick Together	Come together and exercise with your family. Workout activities are for all ages.	Tuesdays: 3:00 P.M., 7:00 P.M. Thursdays: 3:00 P.M., 7:00 P.M. Saturdays: 11:00 A.M.
Extreme	90 minutes of extreme exercise. This is the most difficult class. Adults only.	Mondays: 7:00 A.M., 6:00 P.M. Tuesdays: 7:00 A.M. Wednesdays: 7:00 A.M., 6:00 P.M. Thursdays: 7:00 A.M. Fridays: 7:00 A.M., 6:00 P.M.
First Climb	Learn how to climb in a safe and structured class. Beginners only. Ages 9 and up.	Mondays: 5:00 P.M. Thursdays: 5:00 P.M.
Top of the World	Improve your rock climbing skills. Intermediate level. Ages 9 and up.	Mondays: 6:00 P.M. Thursdays: 6:00 P.M.
Move and Groove	A fitness dance class. Dance to fun music and exercise at the same time! All ages are welcome.	Tuesdays: 4:00 P.M. Thursdays: 4:00 P.M.
Dive In	A swim class for the beginner swimmer.	Mondays: 10:30 A.M. Wednesdays: 10:30 A.M. Saturdays: 9:00 A.M., 10:30 A.M.
Lap Swim	An unstructured time for people to swim at their own speed. Ages 9 and up. Swim lanes 1–3 only.	Monday–Friday: 6:00 A.M.–8:00 P.M. Saturdays: 7:00 A.M.–5:00 P.M.

1 Which class is good for the whole family?
  a All in One
  b Stick Together
  c Extreme
  d Learn to Rock Climb

2 Which class is good for the beginner rock climber?
  a Stick Together
  b Top of the World
  c Move and Groove
  d First Climb

3 Which is the earliest class at the gym?
  a Lap Swim
  b Early Bird
  c Extreme
  d Dive In

4 Which is the most difficult class at the gym?
  a All in One
  b Extreme
  c Top of the World
  d Dive In

5 What is the time for lap swim on Saturdays?
  a 6:00 A.M.
  b 8:00 P.M.
  c 6:00 A.M.–8:00 P.M.
  d 7:00 A.M.–5:00 P.M.

6 Which class has music and dancing?
  a Dive In
  b Move and Groove
  c Top of the World
  d All in One

Part 10   Making Inferences from Dialogues

Read the conversation and the question. Then circle the letter of the best answer.

A: Hello?

B: Hi, Mary! It's Cathy. How are you?

A: Well, I'm a bit sad today.

B: Why?

A: We had to put Fluffy down yesterday.

B: Oh! I'm so sorry to hear that. Why?

A: Well, she was getting really old, and my husband, Robert, found a lump on her leg.

B: Oh. Was it cancer?

A: Yes.

B: They couldn't do anything for her?

A: The cancer was too far along, and she was too old.

B: Are you going to get another cat?

A: Yes, but not right now. Maybe in a few months.

1 **A** and **B** are talking
   a at work.
   b in the car.
   c on the phone.
   d at a store.

2 Who is Fluffy?
   a a cat
   b a dog
   c a vet
   d Mary's husband

3 What happened to Fluffy?
   a Fluffy is at the vet.
   b Fluffy was killed by a car.
   c Fluffy died.
   d Fluffy is downstairs.

4 What does "we had to put Fluffy down" mean?
   a to make an animal sleep
   b to force an animal to eat
   c to make an animal lie down
   d to humanely kill an animal because it is sick

5 What does "they couldn't do anything for her" mean?

a Fluffy was too sick, and they couldn't help her get better.

b Fluffy couldn't walk anymore.

c They didn't have enough money to pay for Fluffy.

d Fluffy couldn't eat anymore.

Part 11 Making Inferences in Fiction

Read the story and the question. Then circle the letter of the part of the story that answers the question.

It was a bright, beautiful sunny day for a boat ride. Tommy and his family were going whale watching off the coast of Maine. Whales were Tommy's most favorite thing in the world. He read lots of books about whales and knew tons of facts about them. His room had posters and stuffed-animal whales all around it. Needless to say, he was so excited to finally see a real whale up close.

As they boarded the boat, Tommy got butterflies in his stomach. At first, everyone on board the boat was along the railing, searching the waters for a whale, but nobody saw one. They searched and searched, and after two hours a lot of the other tourists gave up and went inside the boat's indoor cabin to eat lunch. Tommy begged his mom to let him stay out on the deck to keep looking, and after much discussion, his mother and father decided it would be OK as long as he had his life preserver securely on.

About twenty more minutes passed, and Tommy's stomach started growling, too. He thought that maybe he should go inside for lunch with everyone else. Just as he was leaving to go inside, something caught his eye. He turned and saw the most miraculous sight: a whole family of whales swimming along the side of the boat! They were so close; he thought he could touch them! He leaned over the railing to put his hand out, and he lost his balance and fell in the water. Soon, a baby whale came up to him, and Tommy was now nose to nose with the baby whale! He reached out and pet the whale's head, and he thought he saw the baby whale smile! He was so excited! Before he could reach out again, a rope was thrown down, and he was lifted back into the boat. The whole boatload of people was on the deck cheering for him. He was safe on the deck. He coughed up some water and got his bearings, and when he was finally able to speak, he said, "Throw me back in! I've got a whale to catch!"

1 How old do you think Tommy is?

a 2 years old

b 6 years old

c 20 years old

d 40 years old

2 How was Tommy feeling when he had "butterflies in his stomach"?

    a sick

    b scared

    c excited

    d confused

3 Why did the other tourists go inside the boat cabin?

    a They were tired.

    b They were feeling sick.

    c They were afraid of the whales.

    d There were no whales in the water.

4 When Tommy's stomach was growling, how was Tommy feeling?

    a hungry

    b tired

    c sick

    d angry .

5 When Tommy said, "Throw me back in. I've got a whale to catch!" how was he feeling?

    a He wanted to catch a whale.

    b He was scared, and he didn't want to see any more whales.

    c He was excited, and he wanted to go swimming with the whales again.

    d He wanted to go back to land.

Part 12   Thinking in English

Circle the letter of the correct word to complete the sentence.

1 Susan couldn't go to the park with us. She wasn't feeling _____ .

    a cold

    b well

    c sad

    d ugly

2 Chicago is one of the coldest places in the United States. Winter there usually lasts a long _____ .

    a time

    b year

    c season

    d winter

3 The children were being too loud, and so they got kicked out of the _____ .

    a park

    b library

    c pool

    d trouble

4 John really likes the _____ . He likes to go hiking, fishing, and camping every chance he can get.

 a school

 b indoors

 c nature

 d outdoors

5 When you meet a dog for the first time, let the dog _____ your hand. The dog can tell a lot about your scent.

 a smell

 b bite

 c lick

 d pet

Part 13   Identifying Patterns of Organization

Read the paragraph. Which kind of pattern does it have? Is it a listing pattern, a sequence pattern, or a comparison pattern? Circle the letter of the correct answer.

1 On January 20, 2009, Barack Obama became the 44th President of the United States. He has led an interesting life. In 1961, Barack Obama was born in Honolulu, Hawaii. During part of his childhood, he lived in Indonesia with his family. When he was college-bound, he went to Occidental College for two years and then graduated from Columbia University in 1983. For 3 years, Obama worked as Director of the Developing Communities Project in Chicago. After his years at this job, he began law school at Harvard University. In 1991, with his law degree in hand, he returned to Chicago. While living in Chicago again, he married Michelle Robinson. During their years in Chicago, Obama served as a law professor at the University of Chicago Law School from 1992–2004. While he was in this job, his two daughters were born in 1998 and 2001. He served as a senator of Illinois from 2005–2008 before becoming president in 2009. His run for presidency was a short one compared to others who were president.

 a listing pattern

 b sequence pattern

 c comparison pattern

2 I live in San Francisco, California. It is a beautiful city, and many people come here to sightsee. Whenever friends come to town to visit, I have lots of places to show them. First, I like to begin with the Golden Gate Bridge, the most famous bridge in the world. I like to walk across it, since it now has a great pedestrian walkway. Other attractions many of my visitors like to go to are Fisherman's Wharf and Pier 39. This has a festive market with lots of good places to eat and great places to shop. Union Square is another place for the serious shoppers to go with me. All of the major brands are here along with some more exclusive designer boutiques that sell very expensive, unique items. In addition to these attractions, some of my visitors like to go see Alcatraz, a former prison located on an island right in the bay. If we have time, other attractions include Chinatown, North Beach, and a ride on a cable car. There is so much to do and see in San Francisco. One day is never enough!

a listing pattern

b sequence pattern

c comparison pattern

3 There are many beautiful cities in Europe, but two of the most beautiful and interesting are Venice and Amsterdam. These two cities are often compared, since they both have canals. The people of Venice and Amsterdam decorate the gates to the canals and the ropes alongside them with twinkling white lights that sparkle in the night. In both cities, boats float down the waterways winding in and out of the canals and streets. Besides the canals, Venice and Amsterdam are also alike in their squares. They both have impressive town squares in the middle of the cities. Along the squares, shops, restaurants, and little cafes stand out for the weary traveler and the long-term resident alike. In addition to the canals and the squares, there is a similar feeling in both Venice and Amsterdam—it is a feeling of calm that touches everyone who enters these two stunning cities.

a listing pattern

b sequence pattern

c comparison pattern

VOCABULARY BUILDING

Dictionary Work

USING GUIDE WORDS

Using Guide Words

At the top of every page in the dictionary there are guide words. To find a word in the dictionary, first look at the guide words at the top of the page to know whether you are on the right page or not. Every word on the page falls alphabetically between the two guide words. The guide word on the left side of the page is the starting word, and the guide word on the right side of the page is the last word.

Look at the sample dictionary page below. Find the guide words.

heart attack—heavy duty

heart attack /härt ə-tak/ n A serious medical condition when a person's heart stops working.

heart beat /härt bet/ n The action or the sound of a heart pumping blood through the body.

heavy /he-ve/ adj **1** Things: weighing a lot. **2** People: a nice way to say that someone is fat or overweight.

heavy duty /he-vi-du-te/ adj Something that is very strong and does not damage easily.

The two guide words for this page in the dictionary are: *heart attack* and *heavy duty*. If you are trying to find the word *heat* in the dictionary, you would look at the guide words and ask yourself, "Does this word fall alphabetically between the two guide words, *heart attack* and *heavy duty*?" The answer is yes. You would then continue to look at this page to find the word *heat*.

If you are trying to find the word *hedge*, it would not be on this page of the dictionary, since it falls after *heavy duty* alphabetically.

Practice 1

Look at the guide words. Then circle the letter of the words that would be found on this dictionary page.

1 mess/middle
- **a** message
- **b** milk
- **c** middleman
- **d** meter
- **e** midday
- **f** mild

2 open/opinion
- **a** opponent
- **b** opening
- **c** operate
- **d** optional
- **e** opposite
- **f** operator

3 refuse/regular
- **a** regard
- **b** regulate
- **c** rein
- **d** register
- **e** regret
- **f** rehearse

4 fantastic/fast
- **a** fasten
- **b** farm
- **c** fat
- **d** farce
- **e** fashion
- **f** fatal

5 none/north
- **a** nonstop
- **b** normal
- **c** nominate
- **d** northeast
- **e** noon
- **f** nose

6 piece/pilot
- **a** pin
- **b** pierce
- **c** pillow
- **d** pinch
- **e** pigment
- **f** pine

Practice 2

Look at the guide words in the three boxes. Then write the words in the correct box.

combination	comfort	collar	colony
colt	comic	comma	collide
comedy	column	collect	coma

cold/color	comedian/command	colorful/come

PARTS OF SPEECH

Presentation

Parts of Speech

Knowing the part of speech helps you know how to use the word correctly. Review the parts of speech below:

Noun = person, place, thing, or idea

Verb = an action

Adjective = describes something or someone

Adverb = describes a verb (slowly), expresses time (now, then), manner (happily, easily), degree (less, more, very), direction and place (there, up, down)

Some words can have more than one meaning and more than one part of speech. The dictionary groups the words by parts of speech. See the sample pages below for the word *command*.

command /kə-mand/ n 1) an order that must be obeyed: The boss had many commands for his workers. 2) The total control of a group of people: The teacher did not have full command of his class.

command /kə-mand/ v 1) to tell someone to do something: Our parents commanded us to do our homework.

When reading, if you see a word you do not know, try to figure out how it is used in the sentence. Is it a noun, a verb, an adjective, or an adverb? Trying to figure out the part of speech will help you understand the word.

Practice 1

Look at the underlined word in each sentence. Identify the part of speech of that word. Circle the letter of the correct answer.

1 She read the text <u>quickly</u>.
 a Noun
 b Adjective
 c Verb
 d Adverb

2 He gave the <u>reports</u> to the manager of the store.
 a Noun
 b Adjective
 c Verb
 d Adverb

3 Max is a very <u>hard-working</u> employee.

   a Noun

   b Adjective

   c Verb

   d Adverb

4 They <u>coat</u> their bread with butter.

   a Noun

   b Adjective

   c Verb

   d Adverb

5 They met at the <u>fair</u> last summer.

   a Noun

   b Adjective

   c Verb

   d Adverb

6 The employees took a <u>break</u> at the end of the day.

   a Noun

   b Adjective

   c Verb

   d Adverb

7 Rain <u>delayed</u> the soccer game.

   a Noun

   b Adjective

   c Verb

   d Adverb

8 The teacher was kind and <u>patient</u> with all of her students.

   a Noun

   b Adjective

   c Verb

   d Adverb

Practice 2

Read each sentence and look at the underlined word. Write the underlined word under the correct group.

The price of gas is becoming <u>increasingly</u> more expensive.

The students get three weeks of <u>vacation</u> every summer.

We sat <u>comfortably</u> on the bus tour.

The family likes to <u>vacation</u> at the beach every summer.

Many people <u>successfully</u> get their driver's license on the first try.

Maria doesn't like the <u>taste</u> of salt.

Her son gets <u>anxious</u> at school.

A child's <u>imagination</u> is endless.

The waiter was <u>overly</u> friendly.

The students' grades <u>drop</u> right before an upcoming break.

The fathers <u>coach</u> the team.

The people <u>crowded</u> into the room.

The house was small and <u>neat</u>.

We couldn't find a seat because the theater was so <u>crowded</u>.

Her neighbors are very <u>friendly</u>.

The <u>coach</u> gave the team some advice.

Verb	Adjective	Adverb	Noun

FINDING THE RIGHT MEANING

> **Presentation**
>
> **Words with Different Meanings**
> Many words have more than one meaning. Look at the examples below:
>
> Some words can be both a noun and a verb.
>
> **1.** Here is my <u>report</u>.
>
> **2.** I will <u>report</u> on the news tomorrow.
>
> Some words can be both an adjective and a verb.
>
> **1.** This is the <u>direct</u> route to home.
>
> **2.** Please <u>direct</u> me to the nearest police station.
>
> Some words can be the same part of speech but have a different meaning.
>
> **1.** She is making a lot of <u>progress</u> in class.
>
> **2.** We didn't make much <u>progress</u> up the mountain.

Practice 1

Look at the underlined word. Which is the correct meaning for the word? Circle the letter of the correct answer.

1 There were many <u>objects</u> in the pool.
  a to say you do not like or approve of something
  b things that you can see, hold, and touch

2 The mother bird <u>nursed</u> her baby birds back to health.
  a to take care of
  b someone whose job is to take care of people who are ill or injured

3 Please <u>number</u> the chairs one to ten.
  a to give a number to something that is part of a set
  b a word or sign that represents an amount of something

4 The <u>graphs</u> showed the decrease in sales.
  a to make a drawing that shows a set of measurements or relationships
  b a drawing that shows a set of measurements or relationships

5 Taking tests <u>drains</u> me.
  a to make someone feel very tired
  b a pipe or hole that dirty water or other liquids travel through

6 He was not sure if he was <u>right</u>, but he answered the question.

   a a direction

   b correct

7 The <u>bill</u> was more expensive than she thought it would be.

   a a bird's beak

   b a list of things you have bought and the amount you have to pay for them

8 The fire continued to <u>burn</u> throughout the night.

   a to produce heat and flames

   b an injury or mark caused by fire

Practice 2

Read the question. Circle the correct word to answer the question.

1 Which word means to take a group of people somewhere?

Unfortunately, the bus broke down. Now, we have to bus the people to school by our cars.

2 Which word means to give color to something?

The children like to color during class time. They use all the colors of the rainbow.

3 Which word means to leave a place?

When the bell rings, the students exit quickly. They usually use the exit near the front of the building.

4 Which word means to walk like a soldier?

In March, the troops began to march into the city.

5 Which word means not heavy?

Take the light bag, not the dark one. That one is light. It doesn't have many things in it.

6 Which word means something that is interesting or beautiful to see?

My grandfather is losing his sight. It pains him to not be able to see the beautiful sight of the ocean.

7 Which word means to make a computer or TV do something?

I learned how to program the television so that my favorite TV program is recorded automatically.

8 Which word means to advertise?

The owners of the new market downtown will market their opening day by putting advertisements in the newspaper.

Word Parts

ROOTS, PREFIXES, AND SUFFIXES

Roots, Prefixes, and Suffixes

Some words have different parts. If you know the meaning of some of the parts, you can understand the meaning of the whole word.

A **root** is a part of a base word. A root can make up many words that have a similar meaning.

For example: *loc*ate

Loc is a root meaning *place*. Many words can be made with the root *loc*.

For example: *local, location, locate*

Some common roots:

geo, bio, graph, auto, photo, duc

A **prefix** is a part added before a base word or the root of the word. A prefix changes the meaning of the base word.

For example: *mis*use

Some common prefixes:

dis-, im-, non-, un-, re-, pre-, out-, in-

A **suffix** is a part added after a base word or the root of the word. A suffix changes the meaning of the base word.

For example: use*ful*

Some common suffixes:

-er, -est, -ful, -less, -ly, -ness, -able, -ize, -tion

Practice 1

Look at the list of words. For each group of words, circle the correct prefix and the meaning of the prefix.

1 dishonest, disadvantage, disapprove, disregard
Prefix: un, dis, mis, pre, under, re, non
Meaning: under, not, wrong, before, again

2 antisocial, antibiotic, antifreeze, antivirus
Prefix: un, dis, mis, pre, anti, re, non
Meaning: not, opposite, wrong, before, again

3 irrational, irregular, irrelevant
Prefix: un, dis, mis, pre, ir, re, non
Meaning: under, not, wrong, before, again

4 impossible, improper, impure, immature
Prefix: un, dis, in, pre, under, im, ir
Meaning: under, not, wrong, before, again

5 rewrite, redo, rewind, reappear

Prefix: un, dis, mis, retro, under, re, non

Meaning: under, not, wrong, before, again

6 multicolored, multicultural, multilingual, multinational

Prefix: un, multi, mini, under, mili, non

Meaning: under, not, wrong, many, again

Practice 2

Look at the root and the examples of words with the root. Then circle the letter of the meaning of the root.

1 root: bio

example words: biologist, biology, biography

  a animal

  b life

  c book

  d heart

2 root: pop

example words: popular, population, populate

  a think

  b many

  c people

  d before

3 root: cred

example words: credit, incredible, creed

  a impossible

  b together

  c body

  d believe

4 root: art

example words: artist, artifact, artisan

  a skill

  b art

  c make

  d person

5 root: bene

example words: benefit, benefactor, beneficial

  a happy

  b good

  c show

  d heart

6 root: auto

example words: autograph, automobile, automatic

  a do

  b move

  c self

  d person

Practice 3

Circle the letter of the correct answer.

1 Which suffix can be added on to the root word *paint*?

  a er

  b ist

  c or

  d ful

2 Which suffix can be added on to the root word *simple*?

  a less

  b ful

  c est

  d or

3 Which suffix can be added on to the root word *refuse*?

  a ness

  b ist

  c or

  d al

4 Which suffix can be added on to the root word *end*?

  a ful

  b less

  c y

  d ible

5 Which suffix can be added on to the root word *argue*?

  a ment

  b ly

  c ness

  d est

6 Which suffix can be added on to the root word *introduce*?

  a ize

  b tion

  c ly

  d less

Practice 4

Look at the word. What part(s) does the word have? Circle the letters of the correct answers.

1 enjoyable

  a prefix

  b suffix

  c root

2 unlikely

  a prefix

  b suffix

  c root

3 demand

  a prefix

  b suffix

  c root

4 unusually

  a prefix

  b suffix

  c root

5 preview

  a prefix

  b suffix

  c root

6 logical

  a prefix

  b suffix

  c root

7 unequal

  a prefix

  b suffix

  c root

8 automatically

  a prefix

  b suffix

  c root

WORD FORMS AND FAMILIES

Presentation

Word Forms and Families

A word family is a group of words with the same base word or root. They all are a part of the same family of meaning, but they are different parts of speech.

Look at the examples below:

Root word: Quick

Quick = adjective

Quickness = noun

Quickly = adverb

Quicken = verb

Root word: Strong

Strong = adjective

Strength = noun

Strengthen = verb

You can often tell the part of speech a word is by its suffix. Here are some common suffixes for nouns and adjectives.

Noun: -ion, -y, -ence, -ness

Adjective: -ive, -ful, -ing

Practice 1

Draw lines to match the words with the correct parts of speech.

1 a	true	noun	**5 a**	powerful	noun	
b	truth	adjective	**b**	power	adverb	
c	truly	adverb	**c**	powerfully	adjective	
2 a	seriousness	noun	**6 a**	lengthen	verb	
b	serious	adverb	**b**	length	adverb	
c	seriously	adjective	**c**	lengthily	noun	
3 a	fortunately	noun	**7 a**	excellence	adverb	
b	fortune	adjective	**b**	excel	verb	
c	fortunate	adverb	**c**	excellently	noun	
4 a	pleasantly	adverb	**8 a**	softness	adverb	
b	pleasant	adjective	**b**	soft	noun	
c	pleasantness	noun	**c**	softly	adjective	

Practice 2

Write each word under the correct part of speech.

informative	reflective	promote	beautiful
reflect	destruction	beauty	amusing
inform	promotion	reflection	decisive
decide	destructive	inject	
destroy	injection	information	
permanence	amuse	permanent	

Noun	Adjective	Verb

Practice 3

Read the sentence. What part of speech is the underlined word? Circle the letter of the correct answer.

1 That company is a great <u>employer</u>.
   a noun
   b verb
   c adjective
   d adverb

2 With all of her experience, she is very <u>employable</u>.
   a noun
   b verb
   c adjective
   d adverb

3 The new factory will <u>employ</u> a lot of people in the town.
   a noun
   b verb
   c adjective
   d adverb

4 The mayor of the city is a very <u>influential</u> person.
   a noun
   b verb
   c adjective
   d adverb

5 The teacher was a great <u>influence</u> on the students' lives.
   a noun
   b verb
   c adjective
   d adverb

6 Music can <u>influence</u> young people's lives.
   a noun
   b verb
   c adjective
   d adverb

7 The new teacher has a nice <u>personality</u>.
   a noun
   b verb
   c adjective
   d adverb

8 The doctors <u>personalize</u> their care of their patients.
   a noun
   b verb
   c adjective
   d adverb

9 In order to be a salesperson, you have to be <u>personable</u>.
   a noun
   b verb
   c adjective
   d adverb

Word Forms and Families

Some words have the same form and are spelled the same but are a different part of speech and have a different meaning. Here are some examples of words that are both nouns and verbs.

The <u>score</u> of the soccer game was 3 to 2. (noun)
I <u>score</u> many points. (verb)

The <u>report</u> was due yesterday. (noun)
They <u>report</u> on the status of the project on Mondays. (verb)

The <u>love</u> she had for her dog was strong. (noun)
The families <u>love</u> their dogs. (verb)

To figure out which part of speech the word is, look at where the word is in the sentence and what it does for the sentence. If it is an action word, then it is a verb. If it is a person, place, thing, or idea, then it is a noun.

The pronunciation of a noun is often different from a verb in words with two syllables. For a noun, the stress is on the first syllable. For a verb, the stress is on the second syllable.

object: noun
object: verb

report

visit

shop

rules

objects

pack

projects

Practice 4

Circle the letter of the correct part of speech.

1 There was an <u>increase</u> in production last month.

  a noun
  b verb

2 They usually <u>increase</u> the production at the beginning of the month.

  a noun
  b verb

3 Maria gets a lot of <u>support</u> from her parents.

  a noun
  b verb

4 Maria's parents <u>support</u> her decision.

  a noun
  b verb

5 This machine has only one <u>function</u>.

  a noun
  b verb

6 The machines <u>function</u> on gasoline.

  a noun
  b verb

7 They looked for <u>shelter</u> in the rainstorm.

  a noun
  b verb

8 The trees <u>shelter</u> the plants from the intense sun.

  a noun
  b verb

9 Max's dog is a big <u>comfort</u> to him.

  a noun
  b verb

10 Service dogs <u>comfort</u> the sick children in the hospital.

  a noun
  b verb

11 The two countries had a great <u>exchange</u> of information.

  a noun
  b verb

12 The two countries often <u>exchange</u> information with each other.

  a noun
  b verb

Practice 5

Circle the letter of the correct word.

1 Susan's parents always _____ her decisions.
   a question
   b questionable

2 Susan makes some _____ decisions.
   a question
   b questionable

3 The children were _____ the whole way back home.
   a silence
   b silent

4 The teacher requested _____ during the test.
   a silence
   b silent

5 The workers demanded _____ from their bosses.
   a respect
   b respectable

6 He is not a _____ man.
   a respect
   b respectable

7 This coin collection has a lot of _____ .
   a valuable
   b value

8 My old car is very _____ .
   a valuable
   b value

9 The students want to _____ at getting good grades this semester.
   a succeed
   b success

10 The students owe their _____ to their hard work.
   a succeed
   b success

-ED AND -ING ADJECTIVES

-ed / -ing Adjectives

Some verbs can become adjectives when you add -*ed* or -*ing* to the word. Here are the spelling rules:

If the verb ends in *e*, remove the *e* before adding the ending.

If the verb ends in *y*, you change *y* to *i* before adding -*ed*, or delete *y* when adding -*ing*.

Examples:

bore (verb) + ing = boring (adjective) This is a boring class.

bore (verb) + ed = bored (adjective) I am so bored.

confuse (verb) + ing = confusing (adjective) This is a confusing book.

confuse (verb) + ed = confused (adjective) I am so confused.

Adjectives with -*ing* are the cause of the feeling/situation. Adjectives with -*ed* are the feelings of the person affected.

Example:

This is a boring class. (The class is boring.)

I am so bored. (Feeling)

Practice 1

Circle the correct underlined word.

1 The hike was very tired/tiring. We were all very tired/tiring at the end of the day.

2 Jane's parents were excited/exciting to hear the news of her engagement. The wedding will be very excited/exciting.

3 Tim has four younger brothers. They are all very annoyed/annoying. They play tricks on Tim and hide his things. Tim is very annoyed/annoying.

4 I have had many embarrassed/embarrassing moments in my life. Yesterday, when I was at the pool, I tripped and fell right in the water. I was very embarrassed/embarrassing.

5 Frank has been very stressed at work lately. He usually is a relaxed/relaxing man, but the responsibilities at work are stressful. He needs to go on a relaxed/relaxing vacation.

6 I am very interested/interesting in communication styles. The difference in the way that men and women communicate is very interested/interesting.

Practice 2

Write the correct word to complete each sentence.

| frightening | surprised | satisfying | shocking |
| shocked | worried | satisfied | |

1 When the man jumped from the bridge into the water, we were all _____ .

2 My grades were good this semester. My parents were very _____ with my report card.

3 When Mary walked into the room and everyone yelled "Surprise," she was very _____ .

4 That meal was very _____ . It was delicious.

5 The news of her death was not very _____ . She was old and sick.

6 That old house at the end of the road is _____ . I think it's haunted!

7 My parents are always _____ when I drive at night. They think that there are a lot of bad drivers on the road at that time of day.

Guessing Meaning from Context
WHAT IS CONTEXT?

Presentation

What Is Context?

It is often not necessary to understand every word. Often you can understand the meaning of a word from the context of the reading. The context is the sentences around a word. From the context you can learn:

- the part of speech of a word
- the general meaning of a word

Example:

dress jump sport difficult person try

Swimming is a popular _____ . Swimming became even more popular after Michael Phelps won 8 gold medals in the 2008 Summer Olympics in Beijing.

- Only a noun can follow the words "swimming is a popular…".
- The nouns in the word pool are *dress, sport, person.*
- You need to choose a noun that works with the context of the sentence.

Swimming is not related to a dress, so that is not the best choice. Swimming can't be a person, so that is not the best choice. After you have eliminated all of the nouns, *sport* is the best answer.

Practice 1

Write the correct word to complete each sentence.

immediately	head	began
competitive	met	champion

1 Michael Phelps _____ swimming when he was 7 years old.

2 He was afraid to put his _____ in the water at first, so his coaches told him to start swimming on his back.

3 After he saw the 1996 Summer Olympic Games in Atlanta, Georgia, Michael began to dream of becoming a _____ .

4 He _____ his coach, Bob Bowman, in high school.

5 The coach _____ recognized Michael's talents and strong sense of competition.

6 It was Michael's _____ spirit and dedication to the sport that won him 22 Olympic medals.

Practice 2

Read the sentences. Circle the part of the sentence that explains the underlined word.

1 When I was sick last summer, I was highly <u>contagious</u>. The doctor said that the disease could be passed easily from one person to another. Nobody was allowed into my room. I was very lonely.

2 Angela bought a new <u>outfit</u> yesterday. The clothes are really pretty. They will be perfect for the party this weekend.

3 Charles has a lot of <u>stamina</u>. His physical strength allows him to run for miles. He ran in an ultramarathon the other day. He ran 50 miles in one day!

4 I can't finish my presentation for school tomorrow. There are so many <u>hindrances</u>. My little brother annoys me all the time when I'm studying. My parents ask me so many questions, and my friends keep calling me. The people in my life are making it difficult to get anything done.

5 Thousands of children have <u>obesity</u> in the United States. There are many reasons why they are extremely overweight. The increase of fast food in their diet is the main cause, however.

6 My brother is afraid to speak in front of others because he <u>stammers</u>. He repeats the first sound of every word, and he is embarrassed. He goes to a speech therapist. She helps him with this problem.

Practice 3

Read the sentences. What is the part of speech of the missing word? Circle the letter of the correct answer.

1 The computers at the library are very _____ . They are old, and it takes a long time to go from website to website.
  a verb
  b noun
  c adjective
  d adverb

2 My mother is a librarian. She _____ books and helps visitors find resources.
  a verb
  b noun
  c adjective
  d adverb

3 The new bus line near my house is very _____ . I don't have to walk as far, and so I can sleep in later in the morning.
  a verb
  b noun
  c adjective
  d adverb

4 Samantha knew it was time to get new glasses. She could _____ see the board.

   a verb

   b noun

   c adjective

   d adverb

5 The medical profession is changing a lot lately. The _____ have to comply with insurance company rules and regulations more now.

   a verb

   b noun

   c adjective

   d adverb

6 The Mississippi is a _____ river. The widest part of the Mississippi can be found at Lake Winnibigoshish near Bena, Minnesota. It is wider than 11 miles at that point.

   a verb

   b noun

   c adjective

   d adverb

7 The speaker spoke so _____ that we could barely hear her presentation. She needed a microphone.

   a verb

   b noun

   c adjective

   d adverb

8 My neighbors often _____ about their children. They believe that their children are superior to everyone else's children.

   a verb

   b noun

   c adjective

   d adverb

GUESSING THE MEANING OF WORDS AND PHRASES

Presentation

Guessing the Meaning of Words

The context of the sentences can help you guess the meaning of words you do not know. You may only be able to understand the general meaning of the word, but it will be enough to understand the text.

From the context of the text you may find:

- Information about the word
- A word that has a similar meaning
- A word that has the opposite meaning of the word

Practice 1

Read the sentences. What is the meaning of the underlined word? Circle the letter of the correct answer.

1 The ferry that goes from North Carolina to Bald Head Island is often busy. However, there is an <u>influx</u> of travelers in the summer months. This increase is due to the warm weather and visitors wanting to go to the beach.

   a decrease

   b increase

   c problem

2 Be careful of the street vendors in this part of town. I was <u>swindled</u> by one of them last week. I bought a leather wallet from him. When I got home, I realized that the wallet wasn't real leather. He tricked me into buying it.

   a to be tricked by someone into giving you money

   b to hurt someone

   c to say mean things to someone

3 My little brother came home with a black eye yesterday. He got into a <u>tussle</u> with another kid at school. The teachers saw the fight, and they both got in trouble.

   a trouble

   b a black eye

   c a fight

4 Next week we begin our school projects. We were assigned partners to work with on the project. My partner's name is Claire. I have never worked with Claire before, but I heard that she is <u>genial</u>. I am glad that she is a friendly, happy person; otherwise it would be hard to get the project done!

   a cheerful

   b hard-working

   c shy

5 There are many companies that make the generic product of a popular brand item. You can find everything from <u>generic</u> shampoo to generic dog food. The fact that these products don't have a special name makes them cheaper than the other products.

   a many kinds of products

   b does not have a special name

   c cheap

6 The university hired more office workers to <u>facilitate</u> the increase of new students in the fall. This will make it easier for the office to get the new students into classes so that the semester can begin without any problems.

   a to make it easier

   b to increase in number

   c to begin

Practice 2

Read the sentences. What is the meaning of the underlined word? Circle the letter of the correct answer.

1 After the Revolutionary War, the United States had <u>liberty</u> from British rule. Americans had the freedom to do what they wanted. They did not need to ask for permission from Britain any more.

   a freedom

   b to ask permission

   c to go to war

   d to run a country

2 The magician at the fair was amazing. He <u>levitated</u> a chair right before our eyes. I don't know if it was a trick, but the chair was actually rising and floating above our heads!

   a to lift up

   b to sit in

   c to make something rise and float

   d to perform a magic trick

3 The company's <u>mandate</u> that every employee work on Saturdays was not welcome news. The employees were not happy with this new rule, but they were happy to have a job in this time of uncertainty.

   a worker

   b boss

   c rule

   d news

4 I wasn't trying to <u>mislead</u> you. I just didn't know all of the facts. I really thought the road continued on. I didn't know that the road ended.

   a to make someone believe something that is not true

   b to talk to someone

   c to teach someone the facts about something

   d to give directions

5 That company was a <u>pioneer</u> in touch-screen technology. They were the first to have that technology available to their customers.

   a to have many customers

   b to have a lot of good ideas

   c to be the first to do something

   d to know a lot about technology

6 Ever since he lost the race, he sits around the house and <u>mopes</u>. He makes no effort to see the bright side of things. There are other races, but he prefers to just pity himself.

   a to pity yourself and not make any effort to make things better

   b to lose something that is really important to you

   c to cry uncontrollably

   d to see the bright side of life

Practice 3

Read the passage. Draw a line to match the underlined word with the correct definition.

Linda was an outstanding athlete. She could <u>outrun</u> anyone in any race, and she could beat anyone in any game. She was <u>manic</u> about exercising. She was always excited about exercising. She <u>unfailingly</u> woke up every morning at 5:00 a.m. to run 10 miles and then swim 3 miles in the nearby lake. Some people thought she went <u>overboard</u> with her schedule, but she never thought she was extreme. Her body <u>craved</u> exercise. She wanted to exercise every day, and she was more <u>jubilant</u> after she worked out.

1 outrun		to run faster or farther
2 manic		very happy
3 unfailingly		always do something
4 overboard		behaving in a very excited way
5 crave		to want or need something very badly
6 jubilant		to do something to an extreme

Practice 4

Read the sentences. Then write the correct definition in the blank after each sentence.

strong	to give time or money
funny	do what they are supposed to
to meet	to end someone's work contract

1 My boots are very <u>durable</u>. I wear them all the time and on hikes with very rocky trails. They are still in good condition. _____

2 She has many dogs on her farm. They are great helpers and <u>dutiful</u>. They always do what she asks of them, and they never run away. _____

3 The organization has a lot of great members. They all <u>contribute</u> when the club needs help. Some give money, and others volunteer their time. _____

4 The club <u>convenes</u> every Monday evening at 7 P.M. They discuss ways to increase membership and think of fundraising ideas. _____

5 The teacher doesn't work here anymore. The school <u>fired</u> him, because he wasn't a very good teacher. _____

6 The movie was <u>humorous</u>. We laughed the entire time. _____

Presentation

Guessing the Meaning of Phrases

Phrases are a group of words together. The English language has many phrases. You may not know the meaning of many of these phrases, so you will need to think about the context of the text to figure out the meaning of the phrases. You may only be able to understand the general meaning of the phrase, but often it will be enough to understand the text.

From the context of the text you may find:

- Information about the phrase.
- A word that has a similar meaning.
- A word that has the opposite meaning of the phrase.

Practice 5

Read the sentences. Circle the letter of the correct meaning of the underlined phrase.

1 Although I don't really agree with Sam in general, he <u>has a good point</u> on this particular issue. It makes sense to me.

   a to be wrong

   b to say a fact

   c to be silent

   d to say something sensible

2 I don't trust my friend Susan anymore. She has <u>let me down</u> so many times. She says she is going to do something but then never does it. I can't trust her.

   a to lie to someone

   b to disappoint someone

   c to be mean to someone

   d to ask a favor of someone

3 I don't like to go to my grandma's house. She wakes me up at the <u>crack of dawn</u> every morning. I usually sleep late at my house, but at her house we wake up really early.

   a really late

   b midnight

   c early morning

   d midmorning

4 My brothers <u>are in hot water</u> with my mom again. She is constantly yelling at them. They are such troublemakers.

   a to go swimming

   b to be in trouble

   c to take a hot bath

   d a hot swimming pool

5 Please wear a coat and hat today. I don't want you to <u>catch a cold</u>. You don't want to be sick for the game this weekend.

   a to get tired

   b to throw a ball

   c to get sick

   d to be cold

6 After an argument with John, it's always best to let him <u>cool off</u> before talking to him again. John needs time to stop being angry before he is ready to talk normally again.

   a to become quiet, calm

   b to be cold

   c to be silent

   d to argue

Practice 6

Read the sentences. Circle the letter of the correct meaning of the underlined phrase.

1 Tom works <u>like a dog</u>. He gets up at 6:00 A.M. and works in the field until 7:00 P.M. He only takes 30-minute lunch and dinner breaks.

  a hardworking

  b lazy

  c likes dogs

  d eats fast

2 Henry is nervous today. He is going to <u>ask out</u> Anna. He wants to take her to the movies on Saturday night.

  a to introduce yourself

  b to ask someone their name

  c to ask someone a favor

  d to ask someone to go on a date

3 Many companies use computers to do the work nowadays. The computers can <u>save time</u> since a computer can often do things more quickly than a human.

  a work fast

  b change a clock

  c do something more quickly

  d work hard

4 Since companies began to use computers in their factories, many employees <u>lost their jobs</u>. These people are now without a job, and they don't have the skills needed to get a job in today's business world.

  a to not have your job anymore

  b to not have the skills needed to do a job

  c to lose things at work

  d to not want to work

5 My friends and I are going to <u>go abroad</u> after we graduate from school. We are going to go to Europe first and then possibly to Asia. This will be my first trip to another country.

  a to go to another country

  b to get bigger

  c to finish school

  d to celebrate

6 We usually play our games <u>rain or shine</u>. We hope it's a nice day, but if it rains, we'll still have fun.

  a in any kind of weather

  b a game you play in the rain

  c the players don't have to have shiny shoes

  d whether they win or lose

Practice 7

Read the sentences. Then write the correct definition in the blank after each sentence.

overwhelmed	to talk to
always doing something	faint and fall
learn new things	very different from one another

1 My parents went back to college when they were both 70 years old. They didn't need another degree, but they wanted to <u>stretch their minds</u>. They like to learn new things and keep young. _____

2 My grandmother is always <u>busy as a bee</u>. Every time I go to her house, she is either working in the garden or in her house. She never sits still! _____

3 Katie had a fever at school. It was so hot in the classroom, and Katie felt dizzy. When she tried to stand up, she <u>passed out</u> on the floor. _____

4 My new class at the university is very difficult. It is usually for higher-level students, but the professor let me take the course. I think I am <u>in over my head</u>. _____

5 Trevor's parents are nervous. They can't <u>get hold of him</u>. He's been gone for five hours, and they don't know where he is. _____

6 To compare the two houses was like comparing <u>apples to oranges</u>. They were completely different houses. _____

Practice 8

Read the sentences. Draw a line to match the underlined words to its meaning.

1 Sam was on <u>pins and needles</u> about his grades. He wasn't sure if he passed his classes or not.

to be nervous or anxious

2 We typically <u>run out of time</u> on our vacations. We always have so many things planned, but we're never able to do everything.

to not have any more time

3 The new parents needed to <u>take a break</u>. The baby wasn't a good sleeper, and they needed to rest.

to look like or act like

4 After we graduated from school, my friends and I all promised to <u>keep in touch</u>. I really hope that we can talk often. I don't want to lose our friendships.

to have a rest

5 The children <u>take after</u> their father, Edward. They look a lot like him, and they have his personality!

to talk to regularly

6 The girls like to <u>make up</u> songs. They think of new ones all the time and sing them to their parents.

to invent

Phrases and Collocations

COMMON TYPES OF PHRASES

Common Types of Phrases

There are some words that are often used together. This group of words is called a phrase or a collocation. Knowing common phrases and collocations will help you understand readings.

Here are some common types of phrases:

Verb + Noun: I need to <u>do my homework</u>.

Verb + Adjective: I <u>got upset</u>.

Verb + Adverb: He <u>ignored me completely</u>.

Verb + Preposition (phrasal verb): Please <u>hang up</u> your coat.

Prepositional Phrases: The coffee shop is <u>in front of</u> the school.

Adverbial Phrases: The train is always <u>on time</u>.

Classifiers: I need <u>a pad of paper</u>.

General Collocation: <u>Time goes by</u> quickly.

The best way to get to know phrases and collocations is to read. The more you read, the more you will see words that go together.

Practice 1

Read the sentence. Circle the letter of the correct phrase to complete the sentence.

1 Randy went _____ us in the car. He wanted to get there first so he could set up the camp.
- **a** ahead of
- **b** aside from
- **c** in addition to

2 _____ the steak, Matt didn't like the food at the restaurant.
- **a** Out from
- **b** Near to
- **c** Except for

3 _____ my parents, the celebration was a big success. Everyone had a great time.
- **a** Aside from
- **b** Regardless of
- **c** Thanks to

4 I like to hike _____ to bike. Hiking and biking are my two favorite things to do in my free time.

    a as far as

    b on top of

    c as well as

5 _____ my family, I would like to express our thanks to your organization.

    a In case of

    b On behalf of

    c In front of

6 The flight was canceled _____ the storm. The airline will put us on a different flight tomorrow.

    a out of

    b due to

    c according to

Practice 2

Read the sentence. Write the correct phrase in the blank.

give me a hand	break the record	get over
now and then	run out of money	keep an eye on

1 The players need to _____ their illnesses soon or they won't be able to play in the game on Saturday.

2 Can you _____ my bag while I go to the bathroom, please?

3 The neighbors can _____ if I need help.

4 She talks to her old roommate _____ .

5 It seems that the children only call when they _____ .

6 You need to swim very fast if you want to _____ today.

Practice 3

Read each sentence and decide whether the underlined words form a collocation.

1 That company likes to <u>take a chance</u> on new graduates.

  a yes

  b no

2 We <u>walked to</u> the river and swam around.

  a yes

  b no

3 Next <u>week we are</u> going to the beach.

  a yes

  b no

4 The stores never <u>make a profit</u> on Sundays in that town.

  a yes

  b no

5 We <u>missed the road</u> because we couldn't see in the dark.

  a yes

  b no

6 If we don't leave now, we won't be able to <u>catch the bus</u> to the city.

  a yes

  b no

7 My sisters take a long time to <u>do their hair</u>. I never get a turn to use the bathroom!

  a yes

  b no

8 They <u>danced all</u> night long.

  a yes

  b no

9 My parents rarely <u>get upset</u> at us. We are lucky!

  a yes

  b no

10 Don't tell your secret to Donna. She can't <u>keep a secret</u>.

  a yes

  b no

PHRASES IN CONTEXT

Presentation

Phrases in Context

The English language has many phrases. You may not know the meaning of many of these phrases, so you will need to think about the context of the text to figure out the meaning of the phrases. You may only be able to understand the general meaning of the phrase, but often it will be enough to understand the text.

From the context of the text you may find:

- Information about the phrase
- A word that has a similar meaning
- A word that has the opposite meaning of the phrase

The best way to get to know phrases and collocations is to read. The more you read, the more you will see words that go together.

Here are a few examples of common phrases in English:

> pay a fine
> keep the change
> save energy
> save someone a seat
> go bad
> get married
> free time
> keep in mind

Practice 1

Read the sentences. Underline the phrase in the sentences.

1 Ethan spends money like it is water. He goes to the store every day and buys something.

2 Our parents are very understanding. They tell us to just do our best on the test and to not worry about our grades.

3 Joe should get a haircut before he goes to his interview next week. Employers don't like long hair.

4 Can you have lunch with me tomorrow? I want to ask you a few questions about your job.

5 Those boys in the back of the room always break the rules. They get into trouble every day in class.

6 The Girl Scouts of America organization makes a difference in girls' lives every day. The girls learn so much from being in that club.

7 When you are in the library, don't make a noise. The librarian is very strict.

8 The farmer got up early to milk the cows day in and day out for 40 years.

Practice 2

Circle the letter of the correct phrase to complete the sentence.

1 If you forget to return your library book on time, you have to _____ . It's usually about ten cents a day per book.
  a pay fines
  b give money
  c pay a fine

2 The waiter was so good that we told him to _____ .
  a keep the change
  b have the money
  c save the money

3 Please turn off the lights so we can _____ .
  a keep energy
  b save energy
  c have energy

4 Don't buy any fruit. It _____ quickly.
  a goes bad
  b goes brown
  c is bad

5 I'm going to be late for the concert. Can you _____ ?

  a save me a seat

  b have me a seat

  c use me a seat

6 Chris and Nancy will _____ on Saturday.

  a get married

  b have marriage

  c be marry

7 Firefighters often have a lot of _____ while they are waiting for a call.

  a early time

  b empty time

  c free time

8 Please _____ that the store closes in ten minutes.

  a keep in mind

  b stay in mind

  c be in mind

Practice 3

Choose the correct phrase to complete the sentence. Write your answer in the space provided.

be right back	turn up	hold my friend's place
waste time	get through	come out
save people's lives	catch fire	

1 You only have one week to do this project. I recommend that you don't _____ and get right to work.

2 The stars didn't _____ tonight. There were too many clouds.

3 We need to _____ the volume on the television when my grandfather comes to visit.

4 Did you _____ the whole test? It was so long!

5 She said that she will _____ .

6 Firefighters _____ every day.

7 I need to _____ in line. She went to buy a ticket.

8 Be careful of that candle. You don't want it to _____ !

Practice 4

Write the correct phrase in each blank.

take time	get sick	time passes	waste of time
take a rest	back on track	have lunch	back to work
make a difference	pay the price		

Many doctors agree on one thing: sleep is important! Sleep research shows that if you _____ every day, you won't _____ . If you don't get enough sleep, then your body will _____ . The average amount of sleep needed is 7–8 hours a night. This sleep may seem like a _____ , but you need it!

Not only is a proper night's sleep important, but resting for 15 minutes every day can _____ in how you feel, also. In Spain, the Spaniards take a rest, called a siesta. After they _____ every day, they lie down for about 30 to 60 minutes. After their siesta, they feel rested and ready for work. When they go _____ they feel that their brain got a rest and they are _____ .

Be sure to _____ to get a good night's sleep and a rest every day. As _____ , you will begin to feel healthier and happier and you will have more energy.

Practice 5

Write the correct phrase in each blank.

took a look	got frightened	save money and save time
don't waste	don't worry	save yourself the trouble
have a problem		

Did you get a cut? Burn yourself? If you _____ , chances are there may be a solution right in your very own kitchen.

If you are cooking and you get a cut, _____ and _____ time getting a bandage. Your home remedy is right in the kitchen. Get some black pepper and pour it on your cut. Within a few seconds, the bleeding will stop! One man said that after cutting his finger, he put some pepper on it, and the bleeding stopped immediately. His wife _____ and took him to the hospital. After the nurse _____ at the pepper, she washed it off and the bleeding started again! The man got fed up, walked out of the hospital, and went straight home to get more pepper!

There are many more remedies like the ones here in this article. With these ideas, you will not only _____ , you will also _____ of going to the hospital!

How Words Work in Sentences

IDENTIFYING PARTS OF A SENTENCE

Presentation

Identifying the Parts of a Sentence

In order to understand a sentence, you need to know more than just the words. You need to be able to:

- Find the key parts of a sentence
- Understand what the pronouns in the sentence mean
- Recognize words and phrases that refer to the subject

The key parts of a sentence are:

- Subject (tells who or what the sentence is about)
- Verb (tells what the subject does)

Example:

The dog ran down the street.

The sentence is about a dog. *The dog* is the subject.

The dog ran down the street. *Ran* is the verb. The verb tells us what the dog does.

Practice 1

Write the subject and verb from each sentence in the correct box on p. 133.

1 The television fell off of the shelf.

2 Skiing is very popular in Colorado.

3 Nowadays, many people work from home.

4 That information gave us a great idea.

5 The fire grew because of the oxygen.

6 Behind these trees, a house stands near a lake.

7 The university provides health insurance for every student.

8 A little money buys a lot of things in that country.

money	people	provides	television
work	university	fell	is
information	fire	gave	stands
house	skiing	grew	buys

Subjects	Verbs

Practice 2

Circle the subject and verb of each sentence.

1 My friend works in an animal shelter.

2 Every day, the shelter receives at least 50 new animals.

3 Most of the animals are stray cats and dogs.

4 Sometimes an occasional rare animal, like a snake or a rabbit, comes to the shelter.

5 The work is hard at the shelter.

6 The employees care for the animals.

7 Some animal shelters euthanize, or kill, the animals that are too sick or too old.

8 My friend's shelter is a no-kill facility.

9 She enjoys her work there.

10 People, like my friend, make a difference in these animals' lives.

PERSONAL PRONOUNS AND POSSESSIVE ADJECTIVES

Presentation

Personal Pronouns and Possessive Adjectives

Pronouns are some of the smallest words in the English language, but they are very important. There are two types of personal pronouns.

Personal Pronouns:

Subject Pronouns: I, you, he, she, it, we, they

Object Pronouns: me, you, him, her, it, us, them

A personal pronoun takes the place of a noun or a noun phrase within a sentence.

> **Example:** Did you see Mary? **She** has my keys.

Mary is the subject of sentence #1. The personal pronoun *She* replaces *Mary* in sentence #2. This pronoun is a subject pronoun. The subject is often introduced first, before the personal pronoun is used.

> **Example:** Is Mary at work? I really need to find **her.**

Again, Mary is the subject of sentence #1. In sentence #2, Mary becomes the object of the verb *find*, so the object pronoun *her* is used.

Possessive Adjectives my, your, his, her, its, our, their

A possessive adjective shows that something belongs to someone or something.

> **Example:** She has **my** keys.

The keys are the speaker's, so a possessive adjective is used.

Practice 1

Circle the subject pronouns in each passage.

1 There are many people from all over the world in my class. There is one man from Mexico. His name is Juan. He comes from Mexico City. We usually go out for coffee after school. I really like him. He is cool.

2 There are two women from Japan. Their names are Yuki and Keiko. They didn't know each other before they came to the United States, but they are inseparable. They are always together.

3 There is a woman from Saudi Arabia in my class, too. She is really interesting. Her name is Fariba, and she is really shy. She is coming out of her shell a bit now, but in the beginning, she barely spoke.

4 There is another man from Germany. He is a very funny man. He has a pet monkey, and sometimes he brings it to class. Its name is Harold. I think that is a funny name for a monkey!

5 We do a lot of group projects together in class. Currently we are working on projects about the environment. I am in a group with Juan and Yuki. We are researching wind technology for our project.

6 Fariba and Keiko are in a group together for the project. They did a project in class yesterday on global warming. It was very interesting. They did a great job. We do our project tomorrow. Wish us luck!

Practice 2

Circle the object pronouns in each passage.

1 My summer job is very interesting. Since I am studying to be a nurse, I got a job at a nursing home. This nursing home has about 200 elderly people. Their ages are between 75 and 102. The woman I help is 101! Her name is Rosa, and sometimes I feel she is younger than me! She is so full of life!

2 In the morning, I help Rosa get dressed. She is very stylish. She tells me what to pick out of her closet, and then I help her put them on. She also likes to wear jewelry. She has a lot of bracelets. I put them on her arm. Sometimes she takes them off and rearranges them in a different way. She can be particular! She also has a beautiful wedding ring. She wants me to wash it with soap before I put it on her. She wants it to sparkle! Her husband gave it to her when they got married. He has since died, but she remembers him every day. She carries a picture of him in her purse, and she talks about him all the time. It is very sweet.

3 After Rosa is dressed, I help her into a wheelchair, and we go to the breakfast room. She has many friends, so as soon as we walk into the room, they all call to us. They all want her to sit next to them! She is very popular.

4 I am really enjoying working with Rosa this summer. She is a delightful woman, and I am learning a lot about life from her.

Practice 3

Circle the possessive adjectives in each passage.

1 If you are looking for something different to do this summer, I recommend you go camping! My friends and I went camping at a nearby lake last weekend. We had a lot of fun. To camp, you need to have a lot of things. Luckily, between all of us, we were all set.

2 My friend Sam brought his tent. It is really big, and it has an attached porch. On its roof there is a window so we can see the stars. It is really cool.

3 My friend Michelle brought her camp stove. The stove has two burners, so we were able to have two things cooking at the same time. Her sister brought their family's camp dishes, so we didn't have to eat on paper plates.

4 Our campsite was perfect. Its location is right on the lake, and we were able to swim right from our campsite. The park itself has a lot of activities, too. They have a swimming pool, tennis courts, and a sand volleyball court. Their tennis courts are on top of a hill, so there is always a nice breeze.

5 So, this summer, get your friends and all of their camp gear and go camping. I guarantee you'll have a great time!

Practice 4

Read the passage and identify the subject and object pronouns and possessive adjectives. Then write the pronouns and adjectives in the correct box on p. 137.

Sally was so excited. The morning after her birthday was cool and crisp. It was a perfect day for her first big ride on her new bike. It was the best birthday present ever! She loved it. Sally looked at her watch. She didn't want to keep Tyler waiting at the park.

When Sally arrived at the park, she saw Tyler hanging from the monkey bars. She couldn't see him, but she could hear him singing on the monkey bars. He jumped off them and said, "Hey Sally! Are you ready for our big adventure?" Sally nodded her head, and off they raced down the path behind the park. It was bumpy at first, but Sally felt confident on her new bike.

After they rode for a while, they came upon Fox Lake. It was beautiful at this time of year. The yellow, orange, and red leaves were glowing in the sun. Some of them were on the path, and they made it slippery. They hopped off and dipped their feet in the lake. At first their toes were frozen, but after a while they got used to it, and they were soon in the water up to their knees.

Sally and Tyler stayed there for a couple of hours. They were playing around and looking for wildlife. They saw some snakes, and they found a turtle. They played with it for a while and made a little house for it. After a while they let it go. Sally and Tyler thought they saw it wave its hand as it swam away. Then, Sally's stomach rumbled, and they knew it was lunch time. They hopped back on their bikes and rode back to the park.

At the park, they parted ways for their houses. Sally called out, "Thanks Tyler! That was fun!" Tyler called back, "Let's meet again tomorrow!" As Sally got home, she thought she could eat a horse! All that fresh air and biking made her hungry. She had a great time. She couldn't wait until tomorrow.

They	You	She	his
It	it	him	their
He	them	its	

Subject Pronouns	Possessive Adjectives	Object Pronouns

DEMONSTRATIVE PRONOUNS AND ADJECTIVES; REFERENTS

Demonstrative Pronouns and Adjectives

Another type of pronoun is a demonstrative pronoun. These words replace a phrase or an idea. We use them to refer to something already mentioned (a referent). When they are combined with a noun, they are called demonstrative adjectives.

Demonstrative Pronouns:

Singular: this, that

Plural: these, those

Demonstrative Adjectives:

Singular: this car, that car

Plural: these cars, those cars

Practice 1

Underline the demonstrative pronouns and adjectives in the text.

1 In the United States in the late 1800s, some women began to work for suffrage, or the right to vote. By 1913, there were many women's suffrage groups in the United States. These groups helped pave the way for women to become voters in America.

2 Some supporters of suffrage did many things to have their voices heard. They spoke, wrote, marched, and talked to government officials. There were some supporters that were more extreme in their measures. Those supporters often went on hunger strikes.

3 There were many nonsupporters of women's right to vote. They often threatened women's lives, disrupted their speeches, and destroyed their signs. That was hard on the supporters. These women often felt mistreated and defeated at times.

4 After World War I, more people began to support suffrage for women. By August 1920, women were able to vote in all elections. This is an important part of American history.

5 After the suffrage law went into effect, women began to run in elections. There were many brave women who were the first to be elected officials of the United States government. These paved the way for the many women who are now elected officials in the United States government.

Presentation

Demonstrative Pronouns and Adjectives

Demonstrative pronouns replace a phrase or an idea. We use them to refer to something already mentioned (a referent). When they are combined with a noun, they are called demonstrative adjectives.

Demonstrative Pronouns:

Singular: this, that

Plural: these, those

Demonstrative Adjectives:

Singular: this car, that car

Plural: these cars, those cars

This and *These* are generally used for objects that are close by or ideas in the present time.

That and *Those* are generally used for objects that are far away or ideas in the past time.

Practice 2

Write the demonstrative pronouns and adjectives in the correct sentences.

That	these	This
Those	That support	this reason

1 I am moving, and I have a lot of boxes to pack. _____ over there are already done and can be moved to the new house now.

2 The baby took his first step today. _____ moment brought a lot of happiness to his parents.

3 Traveling abroad is a popular thing to do. There are some countries that require a visa to get in as an American. Many of _____ are in the Middle East.

4 Two years ago, there was a fire in the community theater. _____ building was very old, and its charm is hard to replace.

5 My grandparents supported me a lot during a difficult time in my life. _____ meant a lot to me.

6 I heard that the president of the company was fired. For _____ , I don't want to continue working for them.

Demonstrative Pronouns and Adjectives

Demonstrative pronouns replace a phrase or an idea. We use them to refer to something already mentioned (a referent). When they are combined with a noun, they are called demonstrative adjectives.

Demonstrative Pronouns:

Singular: this, that

Plural: these, those

Demonstrative Adjectives:

Singular: this car, that car

Plural: these cars, those cars

The demonstrative pronoun is used to refer back to something written about earlier.

Example:

> A popular sport nowadays is *high diving*. A high diver jumps from an airplane. While falling through the air, the high diver pulls a cord, and a parachute comes out. *This* can be a dangerous sport if you don't know what you are doing. It is important to learn the right way to do it.

This is the demonstrative pronoun that is referring to *high diving*, which is the referent.

The demonstrative pronoun, *this*, in the fourth sentence refers to the sport, *high diving*, mentioned in the first sentence. It acts as a referent for *high diving*.

The demonstrative adjective is used with a noun. It also refers back to something mentioned earlier in the text.

Example:

> There are some *high divers* who like to free fall. *These people* don't open their parachutes until many minutes into the fall.

These people is the demonstrative adjective that is referring to *high divers*, which is the referent.

Practice 3

Circle the referent for the demonstrative pronoun or demonstrative adjective.

1 Many people think that you have to eat at fancy restaurants in order to get a good meal. There are many street vendors that sell delicious food. <u>These</u> people have some of the best food around.

2 Swimming pools have many rules. A common rule is to not dive in the shallow area of the pool. <u>This</u> is one of the most important rules of the pool.

3 When I was in New Orleans, I heard a great jazz band that played music. They were not a typical jazz band. They had all kinds of instruments. <u>That</u> was some of the best music I have ever heard.

4 The flowers in the botanical garden are from all over the world. In the garden there were some beautiful yellow irises from Japan. <u>Those</u> were beautiful.

5 I really enjoyed my years of living in Paris. The food, the sights, and the scenery were all wonderful. <u>That</u> was a great time in my life.

6 My mother bakes a lot. She makes everything from cookies and cakes to pies and donuts. She wakes up early and bakes all day long. <u>These</u> sweets are delicious!

Practice 4

Circle the referent for the demonstrative pronoun or demonstrative adjective.

1 In the United States in the late 1800s, some women began to work for suffrage, or the right to vote. By 1913, there were many women's suffrage groups in the United States. <u>These</u> groups helped pave the way for women to become voters in America.

2 Some supporters of suffrage did many things to have their voices heard. They spoke, wrote, marched, and talked to government officials. There were some supporters that were more extreme in their ways. <u>Those</u> supporters often went on hunger strikes.

3 There were many nonsupporters of women's right to vote. They often threatened women's lives, disrupted their speeches, and destroyed their signs. <u>That</u> was hard on the supporters. <u>These</u> women often felt mistreated and defeated at times.

4 After World War I, more people began to support suffrage for women. By August 1920, women were able to vote in all elections. <u>This</u> is an important part of American history.

5 After the suffrage law went into effect, women began to run in elections. There were many brave women who were the first to be elected officials of the United States government. <u>These</u> paved the way for the many women who are now elected officials in the United States government.

Vocabulary Building Practice Test

Part 1   Using Guide Words

Look at the guide words. Then circle the letter of the words that would be found on these dictionary pages.

1 carry/case

    a cart

    b cash

    c cast

    d cartoon

    e carve

    f castle

2 impulse/inch

    a incite

    b impulsive

    c inane

    d incorrect

    e inclusive

    f inactive

Part 2   Parts of Speech

Look at the underlined word and identify the part of speech. Circle the letter of the correct answer.

1 He <u>barely</u> knew her before they got married.

    a Noun

    b Adjective

    c Verb

    d Adverb

2 What type of <u>transportation</u> is most popular in your country?

    a Noun

    b Adjective

    c Verb

    d Adverb

3 The picnic basket got wet, and now the sandwiches are <u>soggy</u>.

    a Noun

    b Adjective

    c Verb

    d Adverb

4 Every time I eat hard candy, my tooth <u>aches</u>.

    a Noun

    b Adjective

    c Verb

    d Adverb

Part 3   Finding the Right Meaning

Look at the words in italics. Which is the correct meaning for the words? Circle the word that will give you the correct answer.

1 Which word means *one of the four seasons?* Be careful, many people fall in fall because of the leaves on the ground.

2 Which word means *to plant flowers?* You can always find me in my garden in the mornings. I typically garden before I go to work.

3 Which word means in *good shape?* Sam is not as fit as he used to be. He couldn't fit into his pants.

4 Which word means *with a lot of curves?* I don't like to drive up the windy road when it is windy outside. The car is hard to manage.

Part 4   Roots, Prefixes, and Suffixes

Look at the list of words. For each group of words, choose the correct prefix and the meaning of the prefix.

1 transportation, transport, transatlantic, translate

Prefix: dis, mis, non, re, trans, tri, un

Meaning: again, before, between two things, under, wrong

2 disobey, dishonest, disembark, disarray

Prefix: dis, mis, non, pre, re, trans, un

Meaning: again, before, not, opposite, wrong

3 ex-wife, ex-boyfriend, ex-soccer player

Prefix: dis, ex, mis, non, pre, re, un

Meaning: again, no longer doing/being, under, wrong,

4 subway, substandard, submerse

Prefix: dis, im, in, ir, pre, sub, un

Meaning: again, before, not, under, wrong

5 prewar, prework, preview, premature

Prefix: dis, mis, non, pre, retro, un, under

Meaning: again, before, not, under, wrong

Part 5   Word Forms and Families

Draw a line to match the word with the correct part of speech.

1 a energy   verb   **2 a** recommendation   noun
  b energize   adverb   **b** recommend   adjective
  c energetically   adjective   **c** recommended   verb
  d energetic   noun

Part 6 Participial Adjectives

Write the correct word in each sentence.

interesting	interested	confusing	annoyed
annoying	amazed	confused	

1 My little brother can be very _____ . He bothers me all the time.

2 The train schedule was very _____ . I needed to ask the train conductor.

3 She is very _____ in golfing. She is taking classes next week.

4 I was _____ at how much my niece grew over the summer!

5 I was so _____ with the people in the seats in front of us. They were talking during the movie.

6 Listening to my grandfather speak about his childhood is very _____ to me. I like to learn about the old ways.

7 Sam was very _____ in math class the other day. He didn't understand how to do the problems.

Part 7 Guessing the Meaning of Words

Read the sentence. What is the meaning of the underlined word? Circle the letter of the correct answer.

1 Since there was a <u>shortage</u> of medicine, the doctors had to use it only on the patients who really needed it.

  a too much

  b not enough

  c expensive

2 Tina couldn't take the cooking class this semester since there was a <u>prerequisite</u>. All students have to take Beginning Cooking before they can take the Advanced Cooking class.

  a something that is necessary to do before you can do something else

  b something very advanced

  c something that is very crowded

3 Did you read this article on the problems with the water supply in the world? I thought it was very <u>noteworthy</u>. The world water supply is an important global issue.

  a something that is difficult to solve

  b something that is very boring

  c interesting or important to get your attention

Part 8 Guessing the Meaning of Phrases

Read the sentences and then write the correct definition of the underlined words into the blanks after each sentence.

wait to make a decision	to agree with someone
the best of both choices	very rarely

1 My new roommate and I don't get along at all. We are always arguing. We don't see <u>eye to eye</u> on anything! _____

2 We really can't decide which house to buy. We like them both. We can't <u>sit on the fence</u> for too much longer, though. We need to make this decision before someone else buys them! _____

3 My family can't decide where to go for our vacation. My dad wants to go to Colorado to the mountains. My mom wants to go to Florida to the beaches. I want to go to California. We can get the <u>best of both worlds there</u>. California has both mountains and beaches! _____

4 Cindy's friends were excited but surprised to see her out dancing. She doesn't go out very often anymore, <u>only once in a blue moon</u>. _____

Part 9 Common Types of Phrases

Read the sentence. Circle the letter of the phrase that completes the sentence.

1 I can't make it to class tomorrow. Can you _____ for me, please?
a have notes
b make notes
c take notes

2 That store doesn't take credit cards. You have to _____ to buy anything there.
a give money
b pay cash
c pay money

3 You should never look straight into the sun. You could _____ .
a get blind
b go blind
c make blind

Part 10 Phrases in Context

Write the correct phrase in each blank p. 146.

just in case	quickly as you can	meeting place	too late
make a plan	catch fire	get out	fall asleep
save your life	before you know it	out of control	

Fire is dangerous and should never be played with. In an instant, your whole life can change if a fire gets _____ . There are many reasons for house fires. A curtain that is too close to a candle can _____ instantaneously and _____ , your house is burned to the ground. Cigarettes are often the reason for house fires. Many people _____ while smoking a cigarette. The cigarette drops on the ground or in your bed, and there is little you can do to stop the fire from taking over. The firefighters will try to _____ , but often it is _____ . Even if you are very careful with fire hazards in your house, it is always a good idea to _____ _____ a house fire breaks out. As a family, decide on a _____ . This could be your neighbor's house or a big tree in your yard. Wherever you choose to meet, the important thing is to just _____ as _____ .

Part 11   Demonstrative Pronouns

Write the correct demonstrative pronoun to complete the sentence.

this	Those	these	that

1 We are going to hike over to _____ mountain range. It looks far, but it is closer than you think.

2 I was having trouble writing my presentation, but after reading _____ book, I got some more ideas.

3 _____ people at the party last night were all really nice. I'd like to go out with them again sometime.

4 Do you know what kind of flowers _____ are? I really like the color.

Part 12   Identifying Demonstrative Pronouns and Adjectives; Referents

Circle the referent for the underlined demonstrative pronoun or demonstrative adjective.

1 The Louvre is one of the most famous art museums in the world. The paintings are worth millions. <u>These</u> are some of the most famous in the world.

2 The food at the wedding was delicious. The main meal was really good, but the desserts were out of this world. <u>Those</u> were the highlight!

3 I just finished a class at the university on geology. We learned about a lot of things, but I really liked learning about the rocks and gems. <u>That</u> was the most interesting part.

4 When you are doing research, there are many sites online that can give you information. But don't go to blogs or sites written by other people. <u>These</u> can misinform you.

READING FASTER

Introduction: Strategies for Reading Faster

Strategies for Reading Faster

Sometimes it is important to read slowly and carefully, such as when you are reading instructions or technical or scientific passages. Other kinds of reading materials, such as newspaper articles, can be read more quickly. It is important to be able to adjust your reading speed up and down as needed.

The purpose of this section is to encourage you to read faster. Learning to read faster will help you

- read more efficiently and get the information you need from the text more quickly.
- read more. The more you read, the more your general English skills will improve—not only in reading but also in listening, speaking, and writing.
- focus on the idea and meaning of the whole passage rather than on individual words.

To read faster, follow this advice:

- Don't translate. Try to think in English as you are reading.
- Skip unknown words or try to guess meaning from context.
- Time yourself when you are reading.

Practice the strategies for reading faster. Read the passage, following the instructions. Then go to the Reading Faster Practice activity to answer the comprehension questions.

Instructions for Timed Reading

1. Print a copy of the Reading Rate Table and the Reading Rate Progress Log from the Appendices on pp. 205 and 206.
2. Before you start reading, write your exact start time (minutes and seconds) on the Reading Rate Progress Log.
3. Start the timer.
4. Preview the passage by skimming it quickly.
5. Read the passage, skipping over unknown words or guessing their meaning.
6. Stop the timer and write your exact finish time on the Reading Rate Progress Log.
7. Calculate your reading time (your finish time minus your start time), and check your reading rate on the Reading Rate Table.
8. Make a check mark next to your reading rate on the Reading Rate Progress Log.
9. Check your reading rate progress after a few passages. Your number should get higher. If it does not, challenge yourself to read faster.
10. Answer the comprehension questions in the next activity. Do not look back at the passage. Then write the number of correct answers on the Reading Rate Progress Log.

Where Are the Bees?

Bees are essential to the production of food we eat. Bees make honey, but they also pollinate countless acres of crops, such as strawberries, apples, and onions. About a third of the food we eat is a result of pollination by bees. Unfortunately, bees have been disappearing at an alarming rate and continue to vanish without a trace.

In 2006, beekeepers started reporting about something called Colony Collapse Disorder (CCD). The main sign of CCD is the disappearance of adult honey bees from a hive. Disappearance is the key word here, because beekeepers don't find dead bees. They find no bees other than the queen and the immature bees. In October of 2006, some beekeepers reported that they had lost between 30 and 90 percent of their hives. And nobody knew why.

There were many theories for the disappearance of bees, but not much data to support them. Some people thought that cell phone towers affected the bees' ability to navigate. Others thought that the bees were killed by fungi and bacteria, while another theory blamed climate change. But no one really knew for sure.

The most convincing theory has to do with pesticides and the lifestyle of the bees today. Nowadays, beekeepers get most their revenue not from producing honey but from renting bees to pollinate plants. This means that the life of a typical bee now consists of traveling all around the country to pollinate crops as the seasons change. That means a lot of traveling on trucks, which is very stressful to bees. It is not unusual for up to 30% of the hive to die during transport due to stress. In addition, bees that spend most of their time locked up on trucks are not exposed to nutritious nectar from plants. Instead, they live on a diet of corn syrup, usually genetically modified and loaded with residual pesticides. Finally, bees that are forced to pollinate commercial fields are continuously exposed to powerful pesticides that eventually kill them.

No one knows for sure what causes bees to disappear. Most likely, it is a combination of factors. One thing is clear, though—losing bees is very costly for the economy. Bee pollination services are worth over $8 billion a year, so losing bees will cause these businesses to lose millions. Losing bees may cause farmers in the United States to lose $15 billion, and other businesses to lose $75 billion. With no bees, pollination will have to be done by hand, which would diminish the quality of food and increase food prices.

The productivity of modern agriculture depends on the work of a little bee. We hear a lot about big environmental disasters almost every day. But one of the biggest may just be the loss of that tiny flying insect.

Reading Faster Practice

**Circle the letter of the correct answer based on the reading "Where Are the Bees?"
Write the number of correct answers on the Reading Rate Log.**

1 This passage is about

   a the study of bees.

   b how the life of a typical bee has changed.

   c the disappearance of bees.

2 Colony Collapse Disorder

   a causes bees to disappear.

   b was first reported in 2006.

   c explains why bees are dying.

3 One of the reasons why bees are disappearing might be that they

   a get tired.

   b need to pollinate plants.

   c get poisoned by pesticides.

4 We can infer from this passage that most bees

   a have a poor diet.

   b have lost the ability to produce honey.

   c die during transport.

5 Losing bees will

   a decrease food prices.

   b have costly consequences.

   c contribute to climate change.

6 Pollination by people is

   a as effective as pollination by bees.

   b not as good as pollination by bees.

   c impossible.

Timed Reading Practice

PRACTICE 1   OVERCOMING FEAR
TIMED READING 1

Getting Back on Board
Bethany Hamilton Overcomes Her Fear

American president Franklin D. Roosevelt once said: "The only thing we have to fear is fear itself." This means that there is nothing to be afraid of. Courage takes a lot of mind strength. You have to think through your fears and dismiss them as they come up. You have to understand that to be afraid will only hamper your experience or your ability to do the job. Bethany Hamilton, a professional surfer from Hawaii, knows all about fear and how to overcome it.

On October 31, 2003, at the age of 13, Bethany went surfing with her good friends early in the morning. As she was lying on her surfboard, she dangled her left arm in the water. Soon afterward, a 15-foot tiger shark attacked her, severing her left arm below the shoulder. Her friends took her onto shore and made a tourniquet out of a rope and wrapped it around the stump of her arm. When she arrived at the hospital, she had lost over 60 percent of her blood, and she was in shock. She spent many days in the hospital, where the doctors worked on the area below her shoulder. With one arm, Bethany is now considered an amputee, a person with a missing limb.

Despite the trauma from the shark attack, Bethany was out surfing after six weeks. She used a custom-made board that was longer and thicker and had a handle for her right arm. This makes it easier for her to paddle. She worked hard at learning how to surf with one arm and, within a few months after the shark attack, she continued to compete in major surfing competitions. Bethany said that the only fear she had after the incident was that she wouldn't be able to surf again. Her love and passion for surfing helped her overcome any fear that she had about going back in the water.

Timed Reading 1 Comprehension Questions

Circle the letter of the correct answer to the comprehension question based on Reading 1. Calculate your reading time (your Finish Time minus your Start Time) and check your reading rate on the **Reading Rate Table**. Mark a checkmark next to your reading rate on the **Reading Rate Progress Log.** Check your reading rate progress after a few passages. The number should get higher. If not, challenge yourself to read faster.

1 This passage is about
   a a famous saying about fear.
   b how dangerous tiger sharks can be.
   c how a young surfer overcame her fear.
   d how amputees live.

2 Who said, "The only thing we have to fear is fear itself"?
   a Bethany Hamilton
   b the doctor who helped Bethany
   c Franklin D. Roosevelt
   d Bethany's friends

3 What does the saying "The only thing we have to fear is fear itself" mean?
   a You should be afraid of everything.
   b Being afraid is a terrible thing.
   c There is nothing to be afraid of.
   d Fear is very scary.

4 What was Bethany doing when the tiger shark bit her arm?
   a She was lying on her surfboard.
   b She was surfing a wave.
   c She was paddling out to catch a wave.
   d She was sitting on her surfboard.

5 What did her friends do right after the shark bit her?
   a They took her to the hospital.
   b They made a tourniquet for her arm.
   c They gave her blood.
   d They called the doctor.

6 What was Bethany afraid of after the shark attack?
   a She was afraid of sharks.
   b She was afraid of surfing.
   c She was afraid that she wouldn't be able to walk again.
   d She was afraid that she wouldn't be able to surf again.

Use Your Fear
How Fear Can Help You

Your fear may save your life one day. It did for Theresa Lennon. One day, as Theresa was walking to her car at the shopping mall, a man approached her in the parking lot. He said his car ran out of gas, and he needed a ride to a gas station. Just before Theresa opened her car door for him, she got a funny feeling that this man was dangerous. She quickly ran back inside the mall and alerted a police officer. The police officer later tracked the man down. Theresa's instincts were right. The man had a gun and some rope in his jacket. If Theresa had given this man a ride home, she may not be alive today.

Theresa was lucky, but she was also smart to trust that funny feeling she got when she first met the man in the parking lot. She had sense to act on her fear instead of squelching it. Research on fear shows that victims of violence usually feel a sense of fear before it occurs. Some people don't trust their feelings of fear and think that they are being irrational or foolish. But researchers say that it is important to act on these fears and to not waste time. If you second-guess your fear, then you may lose valuable time.

Animals have a keen sense for danger. An antelope can sense a lion's presence without knowing exactly where it might be stalking. A mouse hides in a hole from a hawk it cannot see. Just like these animals, humans also have these instincts to avoid danger. Fear is a chain reaction in the brain that starts with a stressful stimulus and ends with the release of chemicals that causes your heart to beat fast, your muscles to tense up, and the hair on the back of your neck to stand up. At this point, your brain activates the "fight or flight" response. "Fight" means to get involved in the dangerous situation, and "flight" means to run away. Security experts would say to trust your "flight" instinct. An animal would not explore the situation or dismiss its fears. An animal would run. If you sense something, then listen to your fear and run. It may save your life.

Timed Reading 2 Comprehension Questions

Circle the letter of the correct answer to the comprehension question based on Reading 2. Calculate your reading time (your Finish Time minus your Start Time) and check your reading rate on the **Reading Rate Table**. Mark a checkmark next to your reading rate on the **Reading Rate Progress Log**. Check your reading rate progress after a few passages. The number should get higher. If not, challenge yourself to read faster.

1 This passage is about
  a how fear can hurt you.
  b being careful in parking lots.
  c how fear can help you.
  d why we get scared.

2 Why didn't Theresa help the man in the parking lot?
  a She felt fearful.
  b She didn't have a car.
  c She ran back into the mall.
  d She didn't know him.

3 What do victims of violence usually feel before something bad happens?
  a They don't feel afraid.
  b They trust that everything is OK.
  c They feel a sense of fear.
  d They dismiss their fears.

4 Why don't some people trust their fears?
  a They think they are being irrational and foolish.
  b They think it is a waste of time.
  c They think that it is OK to be afraid.
  d They think they can fight.

5 Why is it important to act on your fears right away?
  a So that you don't waste time.
  b So that you can fight the bad person.
  c So that you can lose valuable time.
  d So that you don't run away.

6 What would an antelope do if it sensed a lion nearby?
  a It would fight the lion.
  b It would run away.
  c It would stalk the lion.
  d It would second-guess its fear.

7 What happens in our brains when we are afraid?
  a Fear gives our brain chemicals, and it makes us feel sick.
  b Our brains get tired.
  c It reacts irrationally.
  d Fear sets off a chain reaction in our brain that releases chemicals.

8 Which physical reaction to fear is not mentioned in the text?
  a heart beats fast
  b muscles tense up
  c hair on back of neck stands up
  d hands get clammy

A Whole New World
Role-Playing Games

You may feel that you lead a humdrum life with a boring job. But certain people know you as a daredevil living an extreme life. How can this be? It is the world of role-playing games. Many people around the world call themselves role-players. They play role-playing games (RPGs) and either create a character or assume an established character to act out adventures. There are many types of RPGs. Medieval fantasy, where the world has castles, knights, and dragons, is one of the most popular types of game settings. But there are many other settings, such as realistic, science fiction, war, and horror.

Nowadays, many of these games are computer or video games, but there are other versions as well, such as live-action role-playing games. In these games, people physically dress up as their character and meet others in their community to act out scenes and situations. Another type is a tabletop version, where people play a board game on a table with miniature characters and dice. *Dungeons and Dragons* is probably the most popular of this type of tabletop role-playing game and is known worldwide.

Invented before the dawn of video and computer games, *Dungeons and Dragons* has been around since its creation in 1974. Gary Gygax and Dave Arneson are the designers of this epic game. It gained popularity immediately, since it was very different from any other board game on the market. One of its many unique features is that it doesn't even require a board. Most of the game's action takes place in the imaginations of the role players. In the game, one player is the Dungeon Master, who holds the secret maps and controls all the characters not chosen by the other players. The other players pick one character and the attributes of that character that are created by dice rolls. The Dungeon Master then leads the players through the quests, battles, and challenges throughout the game. Some players dress up as their characters and act out their situations that occur during the game time.

Timed Reading 1 Comprehension Questions

Circle the letter of the correct answer to the comprehension question based on Reading 1. Calculate your reading time (your Finish Time minus your Start Time) and check your reading rate on the **Reading Rate Table.** Mark a checkmark next to your reading rate on the **Reading Rate Progress Log.** Check your reading rate progress after a few passages. The number should get higher. If not, challenge yourself to read faster.

1 This passage is about
  a acting out a role in a play.
  b theater acting.
  c role-playing games.
  d teacher activities.

2 What is one of the most popular types of game settings?
  a Horror
  b Medieval fantasy
  c Science fiction
  d War

3 What do role-players of live-action RPGs do?
  a Role-players dress up, meet others in person, and act out situations.
  b They play board games with other role-players.
  c The games are acted out on the computer by the role-players.
  d Role-players stay home and play video games alone.

4 What is probably the most popular tabletop RPG?
  a *Dungeon Master*
  b *Medieval Fantasy*
  c *A Whole New World*
  d *Dungeons and Dragons*

5 When playing the tabletop RPG, where does most of the action take place?
  a Most of the action takes place in a castle.
  b Most of the action takes place in the players' imaginations.
  c The action takes place in a dungeon.
  d The action takes place on the game board.

6 What are some of the tasks the Dungeon Master has to perform in *Dungeons and Dragons*?
  a The Dungeon Master leads role-players through quests, battles, and challenges.
  b The Dungeon Master battles other characters.
  c The Dungeon Master doesn't dress up and is bored.
  d The Dungeon Master created the game in 1974.

Learn from Gaming
The Benefits of Role-Playing Games

There are many critics of role-playing games. Some say that they promote witchcraft and encourage youth to commit suicide or perform acts of violence. Others say that they are antisocial and that the people who play them do not know how to interact in the real world. Since this criticism has come forth, there have been numerous studies and surveys conducted on role-playing games. The results of these studies have shown great praise for RPGs, and in fact many benefits of RPGs were found.

Since role-playing games are nontraditional ways of interacting with people, critics believe they are antisocial. Role-players couldn't disagree more with this criticism. One of the main reasons why people play RPGs is for the social aspect to it. Role-players get together weekly to play with their friends in live-action role-playing games or online with their friends around the world. The only reason they play RPGs is to interact with others, so in their opinion, this criticism is simply not true.

There are other benefits to RPGs. The act of role-playing can be a wonderful teaching tool. In countries like Denmark, live-action role-play is a part of the learning process and curriculum in their public schools. Many teachers across the United States also use role-playing in their lesson plans. Some teachers have their students act out a time in history, like the colonial days or during war time. Role-playing not only teaches students the history of that time period but also gives them a taste for what life was like during that time. RPGs also stimulate the imagination—acting out characters helps students think creatively.

Role-playing games can also help people with problem solving. If role-players have conflicts in their lives, they often role-play the situations with their gamer friends to work out a solution to their problems. It is like practice for real-world issues that come up. People are able to try out different solutions during their role-play and see how it feels or how it works out. Role-playing offers a safe environment to explore and figure out real problems and issues.

Don't believe the stigma attached to this type of play. It has many benefits, and it can be a lot of fun. Be a gamer and turn that humdrum life upside down!

Timed Reading 2   Comprehension Questions

Circle the letter of the correct answer to the comprehension question based on Reading 2. Calculate your reading time (your Finish Time minus your Start Time) and check your reading rate on the **Reading Rate Table**. Mark a checkmark next to your reading rate on the **Reading Rate Progress Log**. Check your reading rate progress after a few passages. The number should get higher. If not, challenge yourself to read faster.

1 This passage is about
   a acting out a role in a play.
   b social interaction.
   c the benefits of role-playing games.
   d teacher activities.

2 What criticism of role-playing games is not mentioned in the passage?
   a It encourages youth to commit suicide.
   b It promotes witchcraft.
   c It is antisocial.
   d It is bad for your brain synopses.

3 What do critics of RPGs say about the people who play the games?
   a Role-players do not interact with other people very well.
   b The games are dangerous.
   c The games are bad for their brains.
   d Role-playing is only good for students.

4 What do the results of the surveys say about RPGs?
   a The results were positive and said that there are many benefits to RPGs.
   b The results show that RPGs are bad.
   c The results show that there are not many benefits to RPGs.
   d The results show that many kids become violent after playing RPGs.

5 Why do many people play RPGs?
   a They don't have to talk to people.
   b They like the dress-up clothing.
   c They like to be antisocial.
   d They like the social aspect of the game.

6 How can role-playing be good for students in school?
   a The students learn about technology.
   b The students learn about a time period in a very interesting way.
   c The students do not have to read.
   d The students do not get bored.

7 How do role-playing games help people with problems?
   a They can try out and practice solutions to their problems.
   b They do not have to face their real problems.
   c They can pretend they do not have any problems.
   d They can play games all day.

8 What benefit of RPGs is not mentioned in this passage?
   a RPGs provide practice for real-life issues.
   b RPGs are good teaching tools.
   c RPGs stimulate brain activity.
   d RPGs stimulate the imagination.

PRACTICE 3   BOOKS ON THE BIG SCREEN
TIMED READING 1

Books on the Big Screen
The Book-to-Movie Business

If you read a good book lately, chances are you will be able to see it on the big screen within a year or two. Nowadays, Hollywood takes many bestselling books and makes them into movies. On average, thirty novels are made into movies every year. Hollywood studios often look to the literary world for their next big hit at the movie box office. They believe that if a book was a bestseller, then many of those readers will want to see it on the big screen. In addition, the nonreaders who don't want to read the book will want to see the movie so they can see what everyone is talking about. In short, producers see making a book into a movie as a money-making opportunity.

There are many steps in getting a book made into a movie. First, someone buys the option to make a movie from the book. They contact the author and pay them for the rights to make the book into a movie. The buyer has three years to make the book into a movie, and if after that period of time they don't do it, the rights to the movie go back to the author. The author can then sell the rights to another buyer. Second, somebody writes the screenplay for the movie. The screenplay is the script for the book. The screenwriter writes out the characters' lines and descriptions of the scenes. Third, the actors are hired, and the details of the movie are worked out. Many projects die in this step. It is hard to move out of step three, since it takes a lot of money to hire actors and make movie sets. Last, the movie is made and completed. It is a long process that can take many years to complete.

Whether an author is ultimately happy with the movie version of their book depends on how good the movie is. Authors watch tensely as their stories get adapted and sometimes butchered by the screenwriters, directors, and actors. It is often the case that the book is better than the movie, and both the author and the book's beloved readers are sorely disappointed. Some of the best examples of this are *The Scarlet Letter*, *The Great Gatsby*, and *The Da Vinci Code*. These movies are generally known as bad adaptations of the books. There are many movies that did a great job of representing the book. Some recent examples of these are *Jurassic Park*, *The Godfather*, and *The Help*.

Summertime is known for reading time, since there are not a lot of good movies in the summertime. So read lots this next summer, and you may just get to see your favorite book on the big screen. Hopefully it will make you and the author happy!

Timed Reading 1   Comprehension Questions

Circle the letter of the correct answer to the comprehension question based on Reading 1. Calculate your reading time (your Finish Time minus your Start Time) and check your reading rate on the **Reading Rate Table**. Mark a checkmark next to your reading rate on the **Reading Rate Progress Log**. Check your reading rate progress after a few passages. The number should get higher. If not, challenge yourself to read faster.

1 This passage is about
   a books that get turned into movies.
   b buying the rights to make a movie.
   c authors who write screenplays for movies.
   d books that made bad movies.

2 Why do so many books get made into movies?
   a People like to watch movies more than read books.
   b Movies are easy to make.
   c Movies are more popular than books.
   d Studios believe that if they make a good book into a movie, they can make a lot of money.

3 What is the first step in making a book into a movie?
   a The author writes the book.
   b The actors are hired.
   c Somebody buys the rights to make the book into a movie.
   d Somebody writes the screenplay.

4 In which step do many projects die?
   a the first step
   b the second step
   c the third step
   d the fourth step

5 If the movie doesn't get made after a specified period of time, what happens?
   a The author can never write again.
   b The author gets the rights back and can sell them to somebody else.
   c The author gets to make the movie.
   d The buyer gets money back.

6 Why are many authors not happy?
   a They don't get a lot of money for their book.
   b The movie adaptation of their book is bad.
   c They don't get to choose the actors for the movie.
   d It takes a long time to make a movie.

Not Quite the Same
Why Books Don't Make Good Movies

It happens often: your favorite book is finally coming out as a movie, and you can't wait to see the characters you loved so much in print on the big screen. However, after waiting several years and standing in line at midnight so you can catch the first showing of the movie, you walk out of the movie theater disappointed. The characters weren't the same, many details were missing, and the movie was just not as good as the book. You leave the movie theater feeling cheated and longing for the book again. So many movies fall short of capturing the same magic as the book.

Why do so many movies fail at capturing a good book? Reading a book is a personal experience, and it can be very difficult for directors to live up to the expectations of the books' devoted readers. When we watch an adaptation of a book as a movie, we are getting the director's interpretation of the book. We have to take it as we see it. This can be disappointing to readers who painted the characters one way in their minds. After seeing the movie, however, those personal images are replaced with the movie images.

Another disappointment for readers is that the movies are often different from the book. The director changes scenes or often deletes parts of the book so that the whole story doesn't unfold in the movie. Many of the details of the book are left out of the movie. This is often due to time constraints. It is hard for a screenwriter to make an 800-page book into a two-hour movie.

Some movies do win the respect of the books' loyal fans. Two example of this are the *Harry Potter* and *Twilight* movies. The series were immensely popular. The movies then created a lot of hype and almost hysteria among the readers. The special effects a movie can offer, along with famous actors, can cause these movies to become blockbusters, earning millions of dollars. But avid readers and die-hard fans continue to love their books more than the screen adaptations that follow.

Timed Reading 2   Comprehension Questions

Circle the letter of the correct answer to the comprehension question based on Reading 2. Calculate your reading time (your Finish Time minus your Start Time) and check your reading rate on the **Reading Rate Table**. Mark a checkmark next to your reading rate on the **Reading Rate Progress Log**. Check your reading rate progress after a few passages. The number should get higher. If not, challenge yourself to read faster.

1 This passage is about
  a why movie adaptations are not as good as their books.
  b why movies are not as popular as books.
  c why devoted readers don't go to see their favorite books as movies.
  d why the *Harry Potter* movies were so good.

2 What replaces a reader's image after watching a movie of their favorite book?
  a Their personal images are replaced with the movie images.
  b The movie images are replaced with their personal images.
  c Their bad feelings for the movie replace their good feelings for the book.
  d Their favorite characters are replaced with other characters.

3 When we watch a movie adaptation of a book, whose interpretation do we get?
  a the author's interpretation
  b the reader's interpretation
  c the director's interpretation
  d the moviegoer's interpretation

4 How are the movies different from the books?
  a The characters are different.
  b There are more characters in the movie.
  c The setting is different.
  d Some parts are different, and some are deleted.

5 Why are so many details of a book left out of a movie?
  a The author doesn't want all of the details in the movie.
  b It is hard to make a long book into a two-hour movie.
  c The director thinks the details are not important.
  d The moviegoers don't like details.

6 What reason is not mentioned for winning over a book's loyal fans?
  a the hype around the movie
  b famous actors
  c special effects
  d a good director

STUDY SKILLS

Choosing Words to Learn

> ### Presentation
>
> Choosing Words to Learn
>
> There will be many new words in the texts you read. Since you can't learn them all, you need choose the words to learn. Here are some rules for choosing words:
>
> 1. **Most common words:** Learn the words that are most common. Lists of the 1,000 most common (or most frequently used) words in English can be found on the Internet and are a great resource. Learn these words. They will help you understand better when you read.
>
> 2. **Most useful words:** Learn the words that are the most useful. These include:
>   a) the words you need to know to understand a passage
>   b) words you have seen before and will see again
>   c) words that are related to the subjects you are studying in school
>   d) words that are related to your interests
>   e) words that are related to your job
>
> Guidelines for Choosing Words from a Text
>
> 1. Read the text to the end without stopping.
>
> 2. Read the text again. Underline the new words and write them beside the text or on a different piece of paper.
>
> 3. Find a list of *1,000 Most Frequent Words in English* on the Internet and look for the words. If they are not on the list, ask yourself: Is it important to this text? Have I seen this word before? Is it related to my schoolwork, my job, my interests? If so, then circle it and find the word in the dictionary.
>
> 4. Write the words in your vocabulary notebook. Write the parts of speech, the sample sentences, and the meanings of each word.
>
> 5. Practice reading and saying the words aloud.

Practice 1

Read the text. Choose two new words from the text. Complete a chart for each new word. Write the following information:

1. Word
2. Part of Speech
3. Meaning
4. Sample Sentence

How do you get to work every day? The price of public transportation varies greatly in different cities. Many people like to ride their bikes to work. Cities have laws for sharing the road with bikers. Carpooling is a great way to save money and gas. Some companies allow their employees to work at home so they do not have to commute to work every day.

_____

_____

_____

_____

_____

_____

_____

_____

_____

_____

_____

_____

_____

_____

_____

Practice 2

Read the text. Choose two new words from the text. Complete a chart for each new word. Write the following information:

1. Word
2. Part of Speech
3. Meaning
4. Sample Sentence

American president Franklin D. Roosevelt once said: "The only thing we have to fear is fear itself." This means that there is nothing to be afraid of. Courage takes a lot of mind strength. You have to think through your fears and dismiss them as they come up. You have to understand that to be afraid will only hamper your experience or your ability to do the job. Bethany Hamilton, a professional surfer from Hawaii, knows all about fear and how to overcome it.

_____

_____

_____

_____

_____

_____

_____

_____

_____

_____

_____

_____

_____

Practice 3

Read the text. Choose two new words from the text. Complete a chart for each new word. Write the following information:

1. Word
2. Part of Speech
3. Meaning
4. Sample Sentence

On October 31, 2003, at the age of 13, Bethany went surfing with her good friends early in the morning. As she was lying on her surfboard, she dangled her left arm in the water. Soon afterward, a 15-foot tiger shark attacked her, severing her left arm below her shoulder. Her friends took her onto shore and made a tourniquet out of a rope and wrapped it around the stump of her arm. When she arrived at the hospital, she had lost over 60 percent of her blood, and she was in shock. She spent many days in the hospital, where the doctors worked on the area below her shoulder. With one arm, Bethany is now considered an amputee, a person with a missing limb.

_____

_____

_____

_____

_____

_____

_____

_____

_____

_____

_____

_____

_____

Practice 4

Read the text. Choose two new words from the text. Complete a chart for each new word. Write the following information:

1. Word
2. Part of Speech
3. Meaning
4. Sample Sentence

Despite the trauma from the shark attack, Bethany was out surfing after six weeks. She used a custom-made board that was longer and thicker and that had a handle for her right arm. This makes it easier for her to paddle. She worked hard at learning how to surf with one arm, and within a few months after the shark attack, she continued to compete in major surfing competitions. Bethany said that the only fear she had after the incident was that she wouldn't be able to surf again. Her love and passion for surfing helped her overcome any fear that she had about going back in the water.

_____

_____

_____

_____

_____

_____

_____

_____

_____

_____

_____

_____

_____

Practice 5

Read the text. Choose two new words from the text. Complete a chart for each new word. Write the following information:

1. Word
2. Part of Speech
3. Meaning
4. Sample Sentence

You may feel that you lead a humdrum life with a boring job. But certain people know you as a daredevil living an extreme life. How can this be? It is the world of role-playing games. Many people around the world call themselves role-players. They play role-playing games (RPGs) and either create a character or assume an established character to act out adventures. There are many types of RPGs. Medieval fantasy, where the world has castles, knights and dragons, is one of the most popular types of game settings. But there are many other settings also, such as realistic, science fiction, war, and horror.

_____

_____

_____

_____

_____

_____

_____

_____

_____

_____

_____

_____

_____

_____

Storing and Studying New Words
VOCABULARY NOTEBOOKS

Vocabulary Notebooks

Learning new words helps improve your English. One way to help you learn new words is to have a vocabulary notebook. A vocabulary notebook is a notebook used only for your new words. Put your words in some sort of order (alphabetical, by category, by topic, by date). This will help you find them later.

There are many ways to organize your vocabulary notebook entries. Follow these steps and look at the sample below.

1. Draw a line down the middle of the page.
2. Write the word on the left side of the page.
3. Beside the word, write the part of speech (noun, verb, adjective, adverb).
4. Below the word, write a sample sentence with the word. If needed, write other sentences to make the meaning clear.
5. Write the meaning of the word on the right side of the page.
6. Check the pronunciation, then read the word and the meanings aloud.

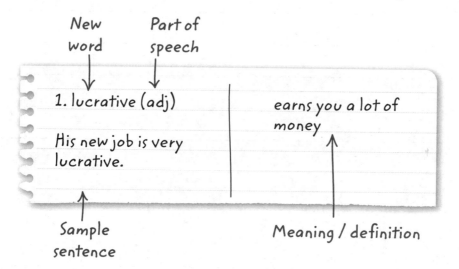

After you write the words in your vocabulary notebook, follow these tips for practicing the words on your own.

1. Put your hand over the meanings. Read the words. Can you remember the meanings? Say them if you can. Review the words and meanings you don't remember.
2. Write the words on a different piece of paper. Can you spell the words correctly? Practice the words you misspelled.
3. Give yourself a "test" many times during the week.
4. Write other sentences with the word.
5. Look for the word in other readings.

Practice 1

Read the text. Choose two new words from the text. Write them on the lines provided as you would in your vocabulary notebook. Include the following information:

Vocabulary Notebook

Word:

Part of speech:

Sample sentence:

Meaning / definition:

Your first year away at college can be exciting. Many first-time students live in college dormitories. These are also referred to as resident halls. In a resident hall, students share small rooms with one or two other students. There usually is a resident hall monitor for each floor of the building. This person makes sure that everyone is following the rules. The resident hall monitor also plans parties and activities for all of the students. There is always something going on. Dormitory life can be a lot of fun!

_____

_____

_____

_____

_____

_____

_____

_____

_____

Practice 2

Read the text. Choose two new words from the text. Write them on the lines provided as you would in your vocabulary notebook. Include the following information:

Vocabulary Notebook

Word:

Part of speech:

Sample sentence:

Meaning / definition:

Mark Twain was a famous writer who wrote novels about young boys named Tom Sawyer and Huckleberry Finn. Mark Twain was not the author's real name. His real name was Samuel Clemens. Clemens was born in 1835 in Missouri. When he was four years old, Clemens's family moved to the town of Hannibal, Missouri. This area became the inspiration for his famous novels. These two novels are some of his best-known works and are still enjoyed by children and adults around the world.

_____

_____

_____

_____

_____

_____

_____

_____

_____

_____

Practice 3

Read the text. Choose two new words from the text. Write them on the lines provided as you would in your vocabulary notebook. Include the following information:

Vocabulary Notebook

Word:

Part of speech:

Sample sentence:

Meaning / definition:

A vegetarian is someone who does not eat meat. There are many reasons people become vegetarians. Some people simply do not like the taste of meat. Others believe it is cruel to eat meat from an animal. Then there are some people whose religion does not allow them to eat meat. Last, there are some people who think that it is unhealthy to eat meat. Vegetarians eat a lot of vegetables, fruit, beans, and soy products, such as tofu. Whatever the reason, the number of vegetarians is increasing all over the world.

_____

_____

_____

_____

_____

_____

_____

_____

_____

_____

_____

_____

WORD MAPS

Word Maps

A word map is a visual organizer that helps you learn a word. It helps you to see the different aspects of the word. Most word maps include a definition, synonyms, antonyms, and sample sentences.

Sample Word Map Template

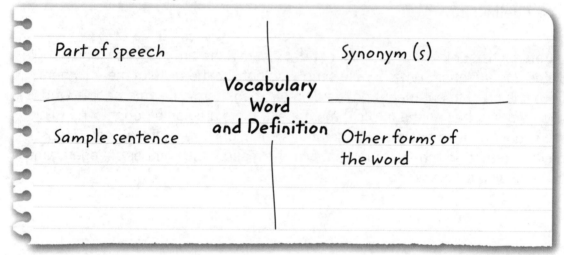

Sample Word Map

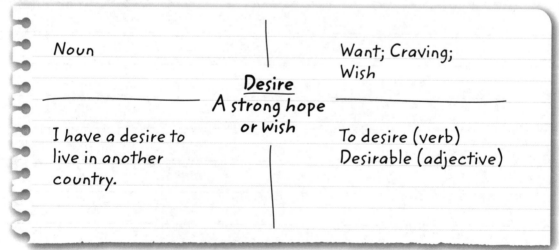

Vocabulary maps can be added to your vocabulary notebooks. They can be used for more difficult words or words that have a lot of synonyms.

Practice 1

Read the text. Choose two new words from the text. Write the information for a word map using the letters A, B, C, D, and E for each section in the word map.

A = Word and definition

B = Part of speech

C = Synonym(s)

D = Sample sentence

E = Other forms of the word

If you have trouble focusing during the day, chances are you are not getting enough sleep. Doctors recommend that people get between seven and nine hours of sleep per night. If you have difficulty sleeping, setting up a bedtime routine can help. Begin with reading or watching a particular TV show, and then after it is over, turn out the lights and go to sleep. Sleep helps you stay healthy both physically and mentally.

_____

_____

_____

_____

_____

_____

_____

_____

_____

_____

_____

_____

_____

Practice 2

Read the text. Choose two new words from the text. Write the information for a word map using the letters A, B, C, D, and E for each section in the word map.

A = Word and definition

B = Part of speech

C = Synonym(s)

D = Sample sentence

E = Other forms of the word

Jake and John are roommates, but they are very different people. Jake gets up at dawn, while John sleeps in every morning until 10 A.M. Jake works hard all day around the house, while John lazes around the house reading and watching television. Jake cooks all of his own meals with fresh ingredients, but John goes to fast-food restaurants or orders pizza every night. Despite their many differences, Jake and John are good friends, and they like living together.

_____

_____

_____

_____

_____

_____

_____

_____

_____

_____

_____

_____

_____

Practice 3

Read the text. Choose two new words from the text. Write the information for a word map using the letters A, B, C, D, and E for each section in the word map.

A = Word and definition

B = Part of speech

C = Synonym(s)

D = Sample sentence

E = Other forms of the word

> Lightning in the sky can be so beautiful. How is lightning created? When you see a bolt of lightning in the sky, you're seeing a giant electrical spark. During storms, electricity builds up in rain clouds. Once in a while, this electricity must find a place to go, so it forms a bolt of electricity called a lightning bolt.

_____

_____

_____

_____

_____

_____

_____

_____

_____

_____

_____

_____

_____

_____

_____

WORD CARDS

Word Cards

Follow the instructions on how to make word cards. Use the cards to study.

1. On one side of a 3 x 5 card, write the word in big letters.
2. In the right corner of the card, write the part of speech.
3. Below the word, write a sample sentence.
4. On the back of the card, write the meaning. Draw a picture, if possible.

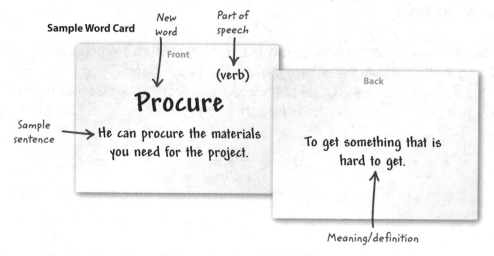

Use your word cards to practice your words. Follow these tips:

1. Look at the front of each card. Say the word aloud and try to remember the meaning. Put the cards with words you don't know in a separate pile. Review those words again.
2. Look at the meaning side of each card. Read the meaning and try to remember the word. Say and spell the word aloud. Check the spelling on the other side. Put the ones you don't know in a separate pile. Review those words again.
3. Practice your words with another student. Test each other by saying the word and asking for the definition or by giving the definition and asking for the word.
4. Make single-sided cards with the word on one card and the meaning on a different card. Write "W" (word) or "M" (meaning) on the back of each card. Play games with the cards.

Word Card Games *(for single-sided word cards)*

Matching Game: *(one, two, or more players)* Put all the cards face up on the table. Match word cards to definition cards. Take turns if more than one player.

Memory Game: *(one, two, or more players)* Put all the cards face down. Pick up a "W" card and an "M" card to see if they match (word with definition). If they don't match, put them back in place. If they do match, put them aside and go again. Take turns if more than one player. The player with the most matches wins.

Sad Jack: *(two or more players)* Use only the word cards. A player picks a card and writes the number of spaces for the letters in the word. The other players guess the letters in the word. For each wrong letter, the player who knows the word draws a part of a face. Face parts can include head, eyes, nose, mouth, ears, hair, etc. If the complete face is drawn before the word is guessed, the drawing player wins.

Password: *(one, two, or more players; two or more teams)* Use only the word cards. One player describes a word to the other players. The player who guesses the word first gets a point. The player/team with the most points wins.

Practice 1

Read the text. Choose two new words from the text. Write them as you would on study cards. Include the following information for each word:

Study Card (front)

Word:

Part of speech:

Sample sentence:

Study Card (back)

Meaning/definition:

> What do you see when you look at the moon? The dark spots on the moon represent different things in different countries. In the United States, people think the shapes look like a man's face. That is how we got the expression "the man in the moon." People in other parts of the world say that these spots make a picture of a rabbit, while others see a woman reading a book. There are many images and stories of the shapes on the moon.

_____

_____

_____

_____

_____

_____

_____

_____

_____

_____

_____

_____

_____

Practice 2

Read the text. Choose two new words from the text. Write them as you would on study cards. Include the following information for each word:

Study Card (front)

Word:

Part of speech:

Sample sentence:

Study Card (back)

Meaning / definition:

Everybody loves popcorn! People have munched on popcorn for thousands of years. Scientists found popped kernels of corn that are more than 5,000 years old. When Christopher Columbus landed in the Americas, he saw Native Americans eating popcorn. He also saw them stringing kernels together to wear as necklaces and hair decorations. Popcorn was popular then and is still popular today.

_____

_____

_____

_____

_____

_____

_____

_____

_____

_____

_____

_____

Practice 3

Read the text. Choose two new words from the text. Write them as you would on study cards. Include the following information for each word:

Study Card (front)

Word:

Part of speech:

Sample sentence:

Study Card (back)

Meaning / definition:

Thanks to two French brothers, Jacques and Joseph Montgolfier, the world has an interesting mode of transportation—the hot air balloon. After lunch one day, the brothers threw their paper bag into the fireplace. Before it burned, the bag filled with smoke and hot air. The brothers watched in amazement as the bag rose up the chimney. This gave them an idea to make more balloons, and eventually they created the very first hot air balloon.

_____

_____

_____

_____

_____

_____

_____

_____

_____

_____

_____

_____

LANGUAGE IN CONTEXT

Practice 1

Part 1

Read the text. Underline the words in the paragraph that appear in the box.

allow	ever	reach	sound
birds	likely	second	
change	most	something	

Have you ever heard a buzzing sound and then saw a flash of something zoom by? Most likely it was a hummingbird. Hummingbirds are the fastest of all birds. Their wings flap between 50 and 60 times a second. These wings allow them to change direction quickly. They have long beaks so they can reach the nectar of flowers. Chances are you won't see one for long. In a second, they are gone!

Part 2

Read the text. Circle the correct answer.

Have you ever heard a buzzing sound and then saw a flash of something zoom by? Most likely it was a hummingbird. Hummingbirds are the fastest of all birds. Their wings flap between 50 and 60 times a second. These wings allow them to change direction quickly. They have long beaks so they can reach the nectar of flowers. Chances are you won't see one for long. In a second, they are gone!

1 Hummingbirds are not the fastest birds in the world.	True	False
2 A hummingbird's wings flap between 50 and 60 times per second.	True	False
3 A hummingbird's wings allow them to change direction quickly.	True	False
4 Hummingbirds have long necks so they can reach the nectar of a flower.	True	False
5 Their beaks reach inside the stem of a flower.	True	False

Part 3

Read each sentence. Circle the letter of the best meaning for the underlined word.

Have you ever heard a buzzing sound and then saw a flash of something zoom by? Most likely it was a hummingbird. Hummingbirds are the fastest of all birds. Their wings flap between 50 and 60 times a second. These wings allow them to change direction quickly. They have long beaks so they can reach the nectar of flowers. Chances are you won't see one for long. In a second, they are gone!

1 Have you ever heard a <u>buzzing</u> sound and then saw a flash of something zoom by?
  a a loud noise
  b a low, continuous sound
  c a quick, high noise
  d a song

2 Have you ever heard a buzzing sound and then saw a flash of something <u>zoom</u> by?
  a walk
  b go slowly
  c go fast
  d sting

3 Their wings <u>flap</u> between 50 and 60 times a second.
  a fly
  b go up and down
  c glide
  d make a sound

4 These wings <u>allow</u> them to change direction quickly.
  a to happen
  b to force up and down
  c to carry forward
  d to make it possible for something to happen

5 These wings allow them to change <u>direction</u> quickly.
  a the way that something is moving
  b the way something sounds
  c the way something is shaped
  d the speed of something

Part 4

Complete each sentence with a word from the box. Write the correct word into the sentence.

buzzing	reach	direction	second
beak	allow	likely	
zoom	flap	sound	

1 The gills on a fish _____ them to breathe under water.

2 The bird was injured. It couldn't _____ its wings.

3 Those kinds of cars go really fast. They _____ by everyone on the race track.

4 Shhh! I think I heard a _____ downstairs. Did you hear it?

5 When I was camping, there was an annoying bee that kept _____ around my head.

6 That was a close race. She beat that boy by one _____ .

7 Can you help me get that vase down from the shelf? I can't _____ it.

8 I'm lost. Do you know which _____ to go next?

9 A bird's _____ reaches into a flower to sip the nectar.

10 Those dark clouds look like rain. It will _____ rain within the hour.

Practice 2

Part 1

Read the text. Underline the words in the paragraph that appear in the box.

begin	doctors	particular	trouble
between	enough	people	
day	night	sleep	

If you have trouble focusing during the day, chances are you are not getting enough sleep. Doctors recommend that people get between seven and nine hours of sleep per night. If you have difficulty sleeping, setting up a bedtime routine can help. Begin with reading or watching a particular TV show, and then after it is over, turn out the lights and go to sleep. Sleep helps you stay healthy both physically and mentally.

Part 2

Read the text. Circle the correct answer.

If you have trouble focusing during the day, chances are you are not getting enough sleep. Doctors recommend that people get between seven and nine hours of sleep per night. If you have difficulty sleeping, setting up a bedtime routine can help. Begin with reading or watching a particular TV show, and then after it is over, turn out the lights and go to sleep. Sleep helps you stay healthy both physically and mentally.

1 If you can't focus during the day, you are getting too much sleep.   True   False

2 Doctors recommend seven to eight hours of sleep per night.   True   False

3 Bedtime routines do not help people get a good night's sleep.   True   False

4 Reading a book and watching TV are two good routines before bed.   True   False

5 Sleep is not important for you mentally or physically.   True   False

Part 3

Read each sentence. Circle the letter of the best meaning for the underlined word.

> If you have trouble focusing during the day, chances are you are not getting enough sleep. Doctors recommend that people get between seven and nine hours of sleep per night. If you have difficulty sleeping, setting up a bedtime routine can help. Begin with reading or watching a particular TV show, and then after it is over, turn out the lights and go to sleep. Sleep helps you stay healthy both physically and mentally.

1 If you have <u>trouble</u> focusing during the day, chances are you are not getting enough sleep.
  a difficulty
  b ease
  c intelligence
  d fear

2 If you have trouble focusing during the day, chances are you are not getting <u>enough</u> sleep.
  a too much
  b too little
  c as much as you need
  d restful

3 Doctors <u>recommend</u> that people get between seven and nine hours of sleep per night.
  a tell
  b suggest
  c mandate
  d praise

4 If you have difficulty sleeping, setting up a bedtime <u>routine</u> can help.
  a a usual way in which you do things
  b nap
  c dance
  d activity

5 Sleep helps you stay healthy both <u>physically</u> and mentally.
  a having to do with psychology
  b having to do with the mind
  c having to do with the body

Part 4

Complete each sentence with a word from the box. Write the correct word into the sentence.

healthy	difficulty	focusing
enough	per	routine
physically	recommend	mentally

1 Students have a hard time _____ a few days before a vacation begins.

2 I have a strict morning _____ . I do the same thing every day.

3 She is having _____ in math class. She can't seem to understand the concepts.

4 Fear is often in your mind. You have to _____ understand that there is nothing to be afraid of.

5 If you go to New York City, I _____ you go to Central Park. There are so many things to do there.

6 Drinking too much coffee is not _____ . It is bad for your body.

7 I am running in a marathon on Saturday. I am _____ prepared. My body is in good shape.

8 We don't have _____ paper to do that project. We'll have to go and buy some more.

9 A cheetah can run fast. It runs 60 miles _____ hour!

Practice 3

Part 1

Read the text. Underline the words that appear in the box.

able	back	horses	many
alone	dogs	human	service
animals	help	love	

We love our pet dogs, cats, and horses. But these animals can do more than just love us back; they can help us in many ways. Animals that help others are called service animals. These animals help people do tasks that they would not be able to do alone. Service animals are not pets but working animals doing a job. Laws state that they can go anywhere a human can go if they are helping a human.

Part 2

Read the text. Circle the correct answer.

We love our pet dogs, cats, and horses. But these animals can do more than just love us back; they can help us in many ways. Animals that help others are called service animals. These animals help people do tasks that they would not be able to do alone. Service animals are not pets but working animals doing a job. Laws state that they can go anywhere a human can go if they are helping a human.

1 Animals cannot help people.	True	False
2 Animals that help people are called service animals.	True	False
3 Service animals help humans do tasks.	True	False
4 Service animals are pets.	True	False
5 Service animals can go anywhere a human goes if they are helping a human.	True	False

Part 3

Read each sentence. Circle the letter of the best meaning for the underlined word.

> We love our pet dogs, cats, and horses. But these animals can do more than just love us back; they can help us in many ways. Animals that help others are called service animals. These animals help people do tasks that they would not be able to do alone. Service animals are not pets but working animals doing a job. Laws state that they can go anywhere a human can go if they are helping a human.

1 But these animals can do more than just love us <u>back</u>; they can help us in many ways.

  a a part of our body

  b the end part of a book

  c to do the same

  d to give someone something

2 Animals that help others are called <u>service</u> animals.

  a tame

  b helping or working

  c hardworking

  d handicapped

3 These animals help people do <u>tasks</u> that they would not be able to do alone.

  a dishes

  b homework

  c walks

  d jobs

4 These animals help people do tasks that they would not be able to do <u>alone</u>.

  a by oneself

  b together

  c with no movement

  d standing up

5 Laws <u>state</u> that they can go anywhere a human can go if they are helping a human.

  a prohibit

  b to give information

  c permit

  d allow

Part 4

Complete each sentence with a word from the box. Write the correct word into the sentence.

back	service	tasks	pets
alone	state	laws	human

1 Chefs have many _____ to do every day. They have to order food, prepare the ingredients, and cook the food.

2 You often see dogs as _____ animals, but have you ever seen a miniature horse helping a person before?

3 The government has many _____ in place to keep communities safe.

4 Even though there are many similarities between monkeys and people, monkeys are animals and not _____ .

5 We have to work on our projects _____ . We can't work together.

6 I love my dog, and I know that he loves me _____ . He is always happy to see me when I get home.

7 That family has so many _____ . They have 3 dogs, 6 cats, and they even have a horse!

8 The documents _____ that it is illegal to prohibit a service animal from entering a building.

Practice 4

Part 1

Read the text. Underline the words in the paragraph that appear in the box.

develop	learn	provide	today
gain	life	school	
important	opportunities	stay	

Today, there are many activities for children to be involved in. Many of these activities are both educational and fun. They can help children develop their talents and learn new skills. Activities can also provide opportunities to learn important life skills, such as discipline and teamwork. Activities can also help kids meet other kids outside of school. Last, activities can help kids stay physically fit. There is a lot to gain from doing activities.

Part 2

Read the text. Circle the correct answer.

Today, there are many activities for children to be involved in. Many of these activities are both educational and fun. They can help children develop their talents and learn new skills. Activities can also provide opportunities to learn important life skills, such as discipline and teamwork. Activities can also help kids meet other kids outside of school. Last, activities can help kids stay physically fit. There is a lot to gain from doing activities.

1	There are not many activities for children to be involved in today.	True	False
2	The activities for children are both educational and fun.	True	False
3	Activities help children develop their talents.	True	False
4	Children don't learn new skills in activities.	True	False
5	Two life skills children learn from activities are discipline and teamwork.	True	False
6	Kids can meet children outside of school while doing activities.	True	False

Part 3

Read each sentence. Circle the letter of the best meaning for the underlined word.

> Today, there are many activities for children to be involved in. Many of these activities are both educational and fun. They can help children develop their talents and learn new skills. Activities can also provide opportunities to learn important life skills, such as discipline and teamwork. Activities can also help kids meet other kids outside of school. Last, activities can help kids stay physically fit. There is a lot to gain from doing activities.

1 Today, there are many <u>activities</u> for children to be involved in.

  a things you work on

  b things you do for fun

  c jobs

  d things you learn

2 Many of these activities are both <u>educational</u> and fun.

  a related to working

  b healthy

  c related to having fun

  d related to teaching and learning

3 They can help children <u>develop</u> their talents and learn new skills.

  a forget

  b make something harder to do

  c want to learn

  d make something better

4 Activities can also <u>provide</u> opportunities to learn important life skills, such as discipline and teamwork.

  a give something to someone

  b take something from someone

  c make something stronger

  d make something more difficult

5 There is a lot to <u>gain</u> from doing activities.

  a forget about

  b get

  c remember

  d lose

Part 4

Complete the sentence with a word from the box. Write the correct word into the sentence.

educational	talents	develop	provide
activities	teamwork	opportunities	gain

1 My children are involved in many _____ after school. My son likes sports, and my, daughter likes art.

2 You can _____ a lot from participating in sports. You learn about self-discipline and teamwork.

3 Swimming is a great sport that helps _____ all of your muscles.

4 Her children are only allowed to watch _____ TV shows. They watch shows that teach them about science and history.

5 Mary has so many _____ . She can sing, dance, and play the piano.

6 Many companies _____ free health insurance for their employees. They even give it to the part-time employees!

7 In a smaller city, there are not as many _____ as there are in larger cities.

8 The number one thing to remember about being on a team is _____ . It's important to work together.

Practice 5

Part 1

Read the text. Underline the words that appear in the box.

again	information	news	reasons
already	last	newspaper	several
current	look	people	work
first			

Many people nowadays get their news from the Internet. There are several reasons for this. First, it is more convenient. Most households have computers or smartphones with Internet capabilities. It is more convenient to look on your computer as you are working than to find a newspaper. Also, the Internet is cheaper. Again, as most people already have Internet access at work or at home, having to buy a newspaper subscription is an additional cost. Last, the Internet is more current. The news sites are able to update people with the most up-to-date information, whereas a newspaper has to wait until the next printing to get the news out. For these reasons, the Internet is taking over as the primary way people get their news.

Part 2

Read the text. Circle the correct answer.

Many people nowadays get their news from the Internet. There are several reasons for this. First, it is more convenient. Most households have computers or smartphones with Internet capabilities. It is more convenient to look on your computer as you are working than to find a newspaper. Also, the Internet is cheaper. Again, as most people already have Internet access at work or at home, having to buy a newspaper subscription is an additional cost. Last, the Internet is more current. The news sites are able to update people with the most up-to-date information, whereas a newspaper has to wait until the next printing to get the news out. For these reasons, the Internet is taking over as the primary way people get their news.

1 Many people get their news from the Internet. — True   False

2 Not many households have Internet access. — True   False

3 Having a newspaper subscription is an added cost. — True   False

4 The Internet is more current than newspapers. — True   False

5 The newspaper is not as up-to-date as the Internet, because it has to wait until the next printing to get the news out. — True   False

Part 3

Read each sentence. Circle the letter of the best meaning for the underlined word.

Many people nowadays get their news from the Internet. There are several reasons for this. First, it is more convenient. Most households have computers or smartphones with Internet capabilities. It is more convenient to look on your computer as you are working than to find a newspaper. Also, the Internet is cheaper. Again, as most people already have Internet access at work or at home, having to buy a newspaper subscription is an additional cost. Last, the Internet is more current. The news sites are able to update people with the most up-to-date information, whereas a newspaper has to wait until the next printing to get the news out. For these reasons, the Internet is taking over as the primary way people get their news.

1 Many people <u>nowadays</u> get their news from the Internet.
  a in the present day
  b at the exact moment
  c in recent days
  d yesterday

2 There are <u>several</u> reasons for this.
  a a lot of
  b different
  c various
  d good

3 Most households have computers or smartphones with Internet <u>capabilities</u>.
  a wiring to a computer
  b the ability to do something
  c to connect to something
  d availability

4 Last, the Internet is more <u>current</u>.
  a easier to get
  b easier to understand
  c expensive
  d happening now

5 The news sites are able to <u>update</u> people with the most up-to-date information, whereas a newspaper has to wait until the next printing to get the news out.
  a to give the most recent information
  b to make a date
  c to make something go higher
  d to write information

6 Again, as most people already have Internet access at work or at home, having to buy a newspaper subscription is an <u>additional</u> cost.

   a math

   b extra

   c putting two things together

   d cheaper

7 For these reasons, the Internet is taking over as the <u>primary</u> way people get their news.

   a main

   b first

   c best

   d only

8 First, it is more <u>convenient</u>.

   a easier to read

   b better

   c easier to use

   d expensive

Part 4

Complete each sentence with a word from the box. Write the correct word into the sentence.

several	capabilities	current	additional
primary	nowadays	convenient	update

1 There are _____ parks near my house. There is one on every corner, it seems.

2 I get my news from the Internet. It's more _____ than the newspaper, since I get the latest news.

3 A lot of people work from home. Computers have made it possible for people to work at home and connect to the office through the Internet _____ .

4 That machine does not have the _____ to do certain functions. We'll have to buy the new one. It can do those functions.

5 Getting my news online is very _____ for me. I'm already on my computer all day, so I can just quickly check the latest headlines without any extra cost or time.

6 My _____ mode of transportation is a bicycle. I ride my bike everywhere.

7 The news channels _____ their headlines every hour.

8 We needed to order _____ chairs. We didn't have enough in our classroom.

Practice 6

Part 1

Read the text. Underline the words that appear in the box.

before	food	popular	things
coins	money	since	today
example	paper	such	

Before we had coins and paper for currency, people used many things for money. One type of popular currency was grains, such as rice and barley. This is understandable, since rice and barley can be eaten, and food is necessary for survival. Other types of currency were animals, such as fish and cows. Again, this is understandable, since these animals can be used for food or milk. In addition to these things needed for survival, there were other more frivolous currencies, such as beads and belts. These were used for decoration, not survival, but nonetheless they were used as money. One final example of money was bat droppings, or guano. Since bat droppings are rich in nutrients, they help plants and crops grow. Bat guano is still sold today, but it is not used as money anymore.

Part 2

Read the text. Circle the correct answer.

Before we had coins and paper for currency, people used many things for money. One type of popular currency was grains, such as rice and barley. This is understandable, since rice and barley can be eaten, and food is necessary for survival. Other types of currency were animals, such as fish and cows. Again, this is understandable, since these animals can be used for food or milk. In addition to these things needed for survival, there were other more frivolous currencies, such as beads and belts. These were used for decoration, not survival, but nonetheless they were used as money. One final example of money was bat droppings, or guano. Since bat droppings are rich in nutrients, they help plants and crops grow. Bat guano is still sold today, but it is not used as money anymore.

1 Before coins, people used many things for money.	True	False
2 Currency means money.	True	False
3 Grains were never a type of currency.	True	False
4 Food often was a type of currency, since food was necessary for survival.	True	False
5 Animals were never used as currency, because they are too big.	True	False
6 Guano is a type of bat.	True	False
7 Bat droppings were valuable, since they helped crops grow.	True	False
8 Decorations, such as beads and belts, were never used as currency.	True	False

Part 3

Read each sentence. Circle the letter of the best meaning for the underlined word.

> Before we had coins and paper for currency, people used many things for money. One type of popular currency was grains, such as rice and barley. This is understandable, since rice and barley can be eaten, and food is necessary for survival. Other types of currency were animals, such as fish and cows. Again, this is understandable, since these animals can be used for food or milk. In addition to these things needed for survival, there were other more frivolous currencies, such as beads and belts. These were used for decoration, not survival, but nonetheless they were used as money. One final example of money was bat droppings, or guano. Since bat droppings are rich in nutrients, they help plants and crops grow. Bat guano is still sold today, but it is not used as money anymore.

1 Before we had coins and paper for <u>currency</u>, people used many things for money.
  a food
  b money
  c decoration
  d coins

2 One type of <u>popular</u> currency was grains, such as rice and barley.
  a easy to find
  b heavy
  c liked by a lot of people
  d delicious

3 This is understandable, since rice and barley can be eaten, and food is <u>necessary</u> for survival.
  a easy
  b wanted
  c hard to find
  d needed

4 This is understandable, since rice and barley can be eaten, and food is necessary for <u>survival</u>.
  a to sleep
  b to live
  c to trade
  d to get money

5 In addition to these things needed for survival, there were other more <u>frivolous</u> currencies, such as beads and belts.
  a beautiful
  b feminine
  c to not be able to be eaten
  d not important

6 These were used for decoration, not survival, but <u>nonetheless</u> they were used as money.

    a in spite of what was said

    b always

    c rarely

    d because of what was said

7 These were used for <u>decoration</u>, not survival, but nonetheless they were used as money.

    a something healthy to eat

    b something pretty you add to make something more beautiful

    c something you can read

    d something you can sleep on

8 Since bat droppings are <u>rich</u> in nutrients, they help plants and crops grow.

    a healthy

    b very expensive

    c having a lot of money

    d containing a lot of something good

Part 4

Complete each sentence with a word from the box. Write the correct word into the sentence.

decorations	necessary	popular	frivolous
currency	nonetheless	rich	survival

1 Do you have all the _____ materials for the project? There are many things we need.

2 This dirt is _____ in iron. The plants grow really well here.

3 You don't need a new couch. You already have one. It would be _____ to buy another one!

4 This style of clothing is very _____ now. Everyone likes it and is wearing it.

5 When you are lost in the forest, the most important thing to think about is

_____ .

6 Did you buy the _____ for the party? I want to make this room look really nice.

7 Rice and barley were types of _____ a long time ago. People used them for money in many different countries.

8 That is a frivolous thing to buy. It's not necessary, but it's pretty, _____ .

APPENDICES

Appendix 1   Taking Notes
Part 1
Underlining and Highlighting

Underlining and highlighting information in a text can help you remember and reference the main ideas and details. Doing something while reading also helps keep you engaged in the text. Here are some tips for underlining and highlighting:

1. Read the entire paragraph before you underline or highlight. After reading the paragraph, decide what the main idea and the details are, and then highlight those parts only.

2. It is not necessary to highlight or underline every word in the main idea or the details. Just highlight the main words that will help you understand the meaning.

3. Use different types of markings. You can underline main ideas; circle important names, dates, and facts; put a star next to key information; or draw a question mark next to any questions you have about the text.

4. Review your highlighted areas before finishing your reading. This review will remind you of the reasons you highlighted the information and what your markings mean.

Part 2
Margin Notes

Another way to help you remember and reference main ideas and details in a text is to write notes in the margin of your text. After reading each paragraph, write key information, such as the main idea, details, names, dates, or facts, in the margin. This can help you in many ways. First, when you take the time to summarize what you just read, you will remember more of the text. Second, your margin notes will be helpful for when you review the information a second time or the next day. Last, your notes will remind you of what you read and will direct you to the important information.

Part 3

Graphic Organizers and Charts

Graphic organizers and charts can help you record, organize, and remember the information you read in a text. Taking the information you read and synthesizing it in a graphic organizer can help you understand the material better. There are many types of graphic organizers you can use to synthesize the information. Here are a few:

1. This simple graphic organizer helps you keep a record of the main ideas and details you read in the text.

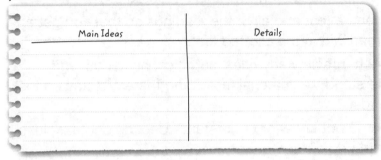

2. This graphic organizer shows the relationship between the main topic, the main ideas, and the supporting details and examples.

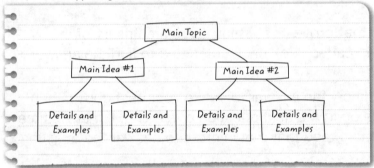

3. This chart can help categorize information and details about the various characters, concepts, or examples in the text.

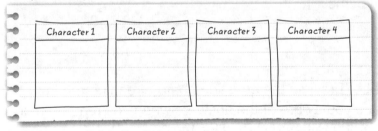

4. This diagram, called the Venn Diagram, can help you compare and contrast characters, concepts, settings, or even two different types of texts.

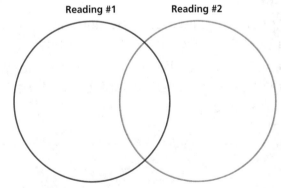

Have an organized notebook or binder for reading so that you can create your graphic organizers for each reading.

Appendix 2   Tips for Reading Tests

Part 1

Budgeting Time

Taking a timed reading test can be stressful. Here are some tips to help you budget your time and get through all of the reading passages successfully:

1. Find out how much time you have for the test and what is expected of you.

2. Before you begin, look over the entire test and all of the readings so that you get an idea of how much you need to read within the allotted time.

3. Before you read the text, be sure to preview any titles, subtitles, headings, and charts. These can help you understand the material faster and therefore stay on task and within the time limits of the test.

4. Do not waste time on words you do not know or understand. Use the context clues to help you with words you do not understand or know.

5. Before answering questions about the text, be sure you read the instructions and each question carefully.

6. When answering questions, use the "prove it" strategy if you are unsure of the answer. In the "prove it" strategy, readers look back at the text to find the answer before choosing how to respond.

7. If there is a question you do not know the answer to, make your best guess, then make a mark next to it and move on to the next question or reading. If there is time at the end of the test, go back and reread that part in order to answer the question again.

8. If you have extra time, go back to the questions you marked as uncertain, then go through the test again if you have time.

Part 2

Previewing Questions

During a reading test, it is important to preview the questions before reading the text. Previewing the questions helps make you aware of the answers when you read them in the text. This will help save you time during timed tests. Use these tips:

1. Preview the questions before reading the text.

2. As you read the text, look for the information in the questions, and underline, highlight, or mark the area of the text with the information from the test question.

3. After you read the entire text, read the questions again. Use the "prove it" strategy if you are unsure of the answer. In the "prove it" strategy, readers look back at the text to find the answer before choosing how to respond.

Part 3
Reading Strategies

There are many strategies you can use to help you become a better reader and understand what you are reading. Engaged readers follow these tips:

1. Preview the material. Get a general idea of the type of reading it is. Is it fiction, nonfiction, or reference material? What subject area does it cover (science, social studies, current events, etc.)?

2. If there are accompanying questions you have to answer after reading, preview the questions before reading.

3. Look over the text before reading it (including the title, subtitles, headings, graphics, pictures, captions, and bold words).

4. Ask questions while reading. Turn headings and subheadings into questions before reading the section so that you are engaged in finding the answers while reading.

5. Highlight, underline, and take margin notes while reading.

6. Make symbols or markings that will help you remember important areas or questions you may have.

7. Stop after every paragraph and reflect, take notes, or highlight the main ideas and details.

8. Evaluate what you are reading. Do you agree with the opinions stated or disagree? How does the information relate to what you know about the topic?

9. Limit your reading time. Do not read for too long. You will not be able to retain the information you read.

10. Control and minimize the distractions around you. Find a quiet spot to read without things that can distract you or take your mind off of your reading.

11. If you find yourself daydreaming and you are not paying attention to what you are reading, take a break, and then reread the area you missed.

12. After reading the text, talk about it with someone, or write your reflection of the material. A discussion or a written reflection can help solidify what you read in your mind.

Appendix 3   Transitions for Patterns

Part 1
Listing Pattern

Many texts list examples, details, and facts. The author uses certain signal words to tell the reader about the list. Some of these signal words include:

- Many
- Several
- A lot of
- Lots of
- Some
- A few

After the author tells the reader about the list, the supporting sentences state the things on the list. These sentences usually start with signal words, such as:

- First, Second, Third. . .
- One
- Other
- Another
- In addition
- Last
- Finally
- And
- Also
- Too
- Yet another
- For example

Part 2

Sequence Pattern

Many texts list a sequence of things that happen in order. Some examples can be a sequence of events, such as events in a person's life, dates in history, etc.

Other sequences relate to steps in a process, such as instructions on how to do something or directions for going somewhere.

The author uses certain signal words to tell the reader that the paragraph will include a sequence. Some of these signal words include:

- History
- Life
- How
- Make
- Do
- Learn
- The way to
- Process
- Steps

After the author tells the reader about the sequence, the supporting sentences state steps or stages in order. These sentences usually start with signal words, such as:

- First, Second, Third . . .
- Before
- Soon
- While
- Now
- At last
- Finally
- When
- At first
- Then
- Now
- Next
- Last

- After
- During
- For a year
- In a month
- The same day
- At this time
- Today
- Last week
- Many years
- Later
- By the 1980s
- Every
- Each

Or the author may just give a date, a time, or the age of a person to signify the place it takes in the sequence.

Part 3

Comparison Pattern

Many texts compare two things, people, or ideas. The author tells us how they are similar, different, or both.

The author uses certain signal words to tell the reader that the paragraph will include a comparison. Some of these signal words include:

- The two things, people, or ideas that will be compared
- Any of the words in the list below

After the author tells the reader about the comparison, the supporting sentences tell about the ways the two things or people are similar or different. These sentences usually have signal words.

For sentences that show how the two things are the same:

- Alike
- Like
- Similar
- Same
- Also
- Both
- Too

For sentences that show how the two things are different:

- Different
- Differ
- Unlike
- But
- However
- While
- On the other hand
- Whereas

For sentences that show a comparison between the two things:

- More than
- Less than
- Bigger
- Smaller
- More beautiful

Appendix 4

Reading Rate Table

All of the passages are about 350–450 words long. To find your reading rate, find the reading time that is closest to yours. Then look across at the reading rate column.

Reading time (minutes)	Reading rate (words per minute)
1:00	600
1:15	480
1:30	400
1:45	343
2:00	300
2:15	267
2:30	240
2:45	218
3:00	200
3:15	184
3:30	171
3:45	160
4:00	150
4:15	141
4:30	133
4:45	126
5:00	120
5:15	114
5:30	109
5:45	104
6:00	100
6:15	96
6:30	92
6:45	89
7:00	85

Appendix 5

Reading Rate Progress Log

Under the Practice and Reading number, write your comprehension score (number of correct answers). Then check your reading rate. Write the date at the bottom of the chart.

Exercise	Intro	P1-R1	P1-R2	P2-R1	P2-R2	P3-R1	P3-R2
Comprehension Score							
Reading rate							
600							
480							
400							
343							
300							
267							
240							
218							
200							
184							
171							
160							
150							
141							
133							
126							
120							
114							
109							
104							
100							
96							
92							
89							
85							
Date							

Part 1 Comprehension Skills

Circle the letter of the correct answer.

1 Look at the picture. What is the article about?
   a school children running a race
   b a woman who won a race
   c best shoes for running
   d how to treat running injuries

2 Read the list below. What is the topic of the list?
   a skiing
   b surfing
   c tennis
   d golf
   e basketball
   f sports
   g soccer
   h football

3 Read the passage below. Is it a paragraph?

When people see a snake, they often run away. There are some, however, run who toward them! These people are called snake catchers, and their job is to catch venomous snakes to either remove them from a public area or extract their venom to make medicine. It is a highly dangerous job. A snake bite from a poisonous snake can be fatal if not treated immediately. Some snakes, like the black mamba, can kill a human within seconds. Snake catchers are taught how to catch and handle a snake so that neither the snake nor the human gets hurt. It's a dangerous job, but it is a necessary one.

a a paragraph
b not a paragraph

4 Read the paragraph below. Choose the correct topic.

When experiencing a headache, many people reach for an aspirin or some other medication that relieves pain. But there are more natural ways to ease the pain of a headache. For hundreds of years, people have used peppermint oil as a way to relieve a headache. Many headaches are produced by stress or tension. It can feel like something is squeezing your head, and the pain runs from one ear to the other. If you apply a little bit of peppermint oil to the top of your head, along your hairline, it will create a cooling feeling that relaxes the muscles in your head and neck. The oil is better for you than aspirin, since it comes from a plant and is all natural.

a stress and how it can produce headaches
b peppermint oil as a natural way to cure headaches
c natural remedies that make you feel better
d how to get cool on a hot day

5 Read the paragraph. Choose the main idea.

There are many famous women in the world, but one of the most famous happens to be one in a painting. *The Mona Lisa* was painted by the great artist Leonardo da Vinci sometime between 1503 and 1505. Nobody knows who the woman was in the picture, or if she was even a real woman. Some people say that da Vinci painted a female form of himself, but most believe the woman in the picture to be Lisa Gherardini. Nobody knows why da Vinci chose her to paint, or if she was a friend or a stranger. The original name is actually spelled Monna Lisa, since Monna is a shortened word for Madonna, meaning "my lady." But, throughout time, the spelling changed to just have one "n." It is the most famous painting in the history of art and continues to inspire oil paintings and art collectors around the world.

a Leonardo da Vinci
b art history
c *The Mona Lisa*
d the spelling of *The Mona Lisa*

Part 2 Comprehension Skills

Read the paragraph and sentences. Then write the number of the sentences in the correct box.

Silk is one of the strongest and softest materials in the world. It is made by some of the smallest creatures on earth. Silkworms are caterpillars that build cocoons made of silk threads. Not only is silk very soft; but it is also very durable. It is known to be the toughest type of material around. Silk fabric was invented in China and played an important role in its culture and economy for thousands of years. It was used not only for clothing but also for paper, fishing lines, bowstrings, and canvas for painting. It is one of the most popular fabrics today.

1 It is made by some of the smallest creatures on earth.

2 It is one of the most popular fabrics today.

3 It is known to be the toughest type of material around.

4 Silkworms are caterpillars that build cocoons made of silk threads.

5 Silk is one of the strongest and softest materials in the world.

6 It was used not only for clothing but also for paper, fishing lines, bowstrings, and canvas for painting.

7 Silk fabric was invented in China and played an important role in its culture and economy for thousands of years.

8 Not only is silk very soft; but it is also very durable.

Main Idea	Supporting Details

Part 3 Comprehension Skills

Scan the information. Circle the letter of the correct answer.

REALTY

Apartment for Rent

2489 Main Street, Apartment J
1 bedroom, 1 bath, near downtown
$800 per month
No pets

Call: 555-8999

Apartment for Rent

222 West Lake Drive
3 bedrooms, 2 baths, in beautiful Brookfield
15 minute drive to downtown
Swimming pool, tennis courts
$650 per month
Perfect for small family, small pets allowed

Call 555-0142

House for Rent

278 Cherry Street
5 bedrooms, 2.5 baths, in quiet neighborhood
30 minutes from downtown
$900 per month
Large fenced-in yard, great for big families, pets OK
Call: 555-0986

Home for Sale

103 Fawn Court
3 bedrooms, 2 baths,
near highway 55
Small backyard
$140,000
20 minutes from downtown
Call: 555-0326

1 How much is the apartment per month on West Lake Drive?

a $800 per month

b $650 per month

c $900 per month

d $140,000

2 Which place does not allow pets?

a 222 West Lake Drive

b 278 Cherry Street

c 2489 Main Street

d 103 Fawn Court

Part 4 Comprehension Skills

Read the dialog. Circle the letter of the correct answer.

A: Did you get it?

B: Yes! I start on Monday.

A: How exciting! What do you have to do?

B: I'm the hostess. I take the dinner reservations and take people to their tables.

A: That sounds like fun. Does it pay well?

B: Not bad. $10 an hour.

A: Wow! That's great! Are they still hiring?

B: You should check it out.

A: It would be fun to work together!

1 What did **B** get?

  a a job

  b a reservation

  c a table

  d $10

2 Where will **B** be working?

  a at a school

  b at home

  c at a restaurant

  d at a store

Part 5 Comprehension Skills

Read each paragraph. Circle the letter of the pattern of organization for each paragraph.

1 Since coal, oil, and natural gas are nonrenewable energy sources, we need to find more renewable energy sources so that we never run out of energy. One type of renewable energy is sunlight, or solar energy. This can be used directly for heating and lighting homes and other buildings. Another type of renewable energy source is wind. The energy from the wind is captured from big windmills or wind turbines. This can help generate electricity. In addition to the sun and the wind, water is a common source of energy. Moving water can help make electricity. Other types of renewable energy include geothermal and hydrogen. These both are taken from Earth and used as energy. We need to think more about these types of energy sources so that our planet stays healthy.

  a comparison pattern

  b sequence pattern

  c listing pattern

2 Driving is a big responsibility. Some people take it too lightly, and, as a consequence, people can get killed. There are steps to driving safely. These steps should be followed every time you get behind a wheel. The first step is to stay focused. Be sure you keep your mind on the road and do not get distracted by other people in the car. Second, keep both hands on the wheel. Placing your hands at the 10 and 2 positions of a clock helps you be prepared for whatever happens on the road ahead of you. While you are driving, be sure to keep your eyes moving. Continuously look in your mirrors and scan the road ahead and behind you, watching for hazards. This helps you anticipate problems that may come up. Next, stay alert. If you get tired, pull over and either get something to drink, eat some food, or get some rest. Last, drive the speed limit. Speeding can be dangerous, but going too slowly can also be dangerous. Be sure to drive the speed limit, and you will be fine.

a comparison pattern
b sequence pattern
c listing pattern

3 Our solar system has eight planets, but out of these Mars is often thought of as the planet most like Earth. Even though Mars is much smaller than Earth, there are many similarities. Both Mars and Earth have a 24-hour day. Another way they are similar is that Mars has seasons. However, the seasons on Mars last twice as long as they do on Earth. Humans could never live on Mars without a spacesuit due to its temperatures. Mars is much colder than Earth, and it would be impossible to live there without protection. The atmosphere on Mars is thinner than Earth's atmosphere. This means that the air is poisonous to breathe. In some ways Mars is similar to Earth, but in more ways it is different, and we would never survive there without our technology.

a comparison pattern
b sequence pattern
c listing pattern

Part 6 Vocabulary Building

Read each question. Circle the letter of the correct answer.

1 What is the root of the word *disorderly*?

  a dis   **c** ly
  b order   **d** disorder

2 What does the prefix *re-* in the word *retake* mean?

  a under   **c** before
  b not   **d** again

3 The suffix *-ness* changes the part of speech of a word. What part of speech is the word *happiness*?

  a noun   **c** adjective
  b verb   **d** adverb

Part 7 Vocabulary Building

Circle the letter of the correct word or phrase.

1 I never was able to figure out the directions. After 2 hours of trying, I was
so _____ . The directions were so _____ .

   a confused, confusing

   b confusing, confused

2 I didn't do my homework last night. I hope the teacher doesn't _____ me to
answer a question.

   a call for

   b call in

   c call on

Part 8 Vocabulary Building

Circle the letter of the word or phrase that has the same meaning as the underlined text.

1 Continuously look in your mirrors and scan the road ahead and behind you, watching
for <u>hazards</u>.

   a dangers

   b holes

   c people

   d trees

2 When you come to school, you have to hang up your coat and then <u>take a seat</u>. Be
sure to sit in a place so that you can see the board.

   a move a chair

   b pick up a chair

   c sit down in a chair

   d steal a chair

Part 9   Vocabulary Building

Read the sentence. Write the subject and the verb in the correct box.

The schools contract the workers to do the job.

Remember, the data inform us of their needs.

The principal contacted all of the parents last night.

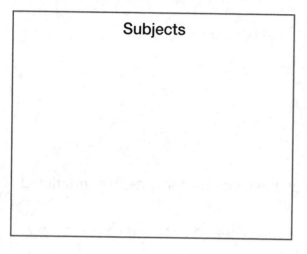

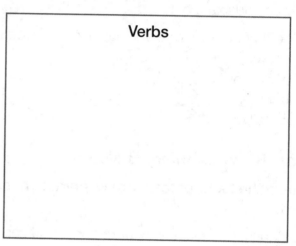

Subjects	Verbs

Part 10   Vocabulary Building

Read the passage. Draw a circle around the subject pronouns, draw a box around the object pronouns, and underline the possessive adjectives.

My family owns an Italian restaurant. My grandmother is from Italy, so we use all of her recipes for the dishes. She does most of the cooking, and it is really good. Our favorite is lasagna. She makes it with sausage and a lot of cheese. My cousins are the waiters. Their names are Alberto and Roberto. They speak Italian to the customers, and all the girls love them. My sister is the hostess. She doesn't like to do the job, but my parents want her to work. She is lazy and talks to her boyfriend all day long on the phone. My parents don't like him. His parents are from a different part of Italy, and they don't get along. I am too young to work at the restaurant, but sometimes they let me pass out bread to the customers. We have the best garlic bread in town. Everybody loves it! Last year, the city gave us an award for the best Italian restaurant in town. That made us so happy!

Part 11   Vocabulary Building

Write the correct demonstrative pronouns and adjectives to complete each sentence.

these	those	that	this

1 I really like _____ dress here. Feel the material. It's so soft!

2 Look at _____ boys over there. They are going to get hurt if they aren't careful!

3 Did you see _____ car go by? It was really cool!

4 Can you help me? Please take _____ boxes that I'm holding to my car.

Part 12   Vocabulary Building

Circle the letter of the correct referent for the underlined pronoun below.

Last year, the city gave us an award for the best Italian restaurant in town. <u>That</u> made us so happy!

a the Italian restaurant

b getting an award

c the city

Part 13   Language in Context

Read the passage. Then read the sentence. Circle the letter of the best meaning for the underlined word.

Driving is a big responsibility. Some people take it too lightly, and, as a consequence, people can get killed. There are steps to driving safely. These steps should be followed every time you get behind a wheel. The first step is to stay focused. Be sure you keep your mind on the road and do not get distracted by other people in the car. Second, keep both hands on the wheel. Placing your hands at the 10 and 2 positions of a clock helps you be prepared for whatever happens on the road ahead of you. While you are driving, be sure to keep your eyes moving. Continuously look in your mirrors and scan the road ahead and behind you, watching for hazards. This helps you anticipate problems that may come up. Next, stay alert. If you get tired, pull over and either get something to drink, eat some food, or get some rest. Last, drive the speed limit. Speeding can be dangerous, but going too slowly can also be dangerous. Be sure to drive the speed limit, and you will be fine.

1 Some people take it too <u>lightly</u>, and, as a consequence, people can get killed.

   a bright

   b like a feather

   c not heavy

   d not seriously

2 Be sure you <u>keep your mind</u> on the road and do not get distracted by other people in the car.

   a focus

   b remember

   c have a good memory

   d choose carefully

3 This helps you <u>anticipate</u> problems that may come up.

   a have

   b find

   c think about

   d expect

Part 14 Language in Context

Read the passage. Then complete each sentence with a word from the box by writing the correct word into the sentence.

The city officials proposed designated areas for graffiti artists to express their artistic talents. For the most part, graffiti artists like the idea, but some are against it. These critics feel that the control of the city takes away their freedom of expression and choice of what they paint. However, most everyone else loves the idea. Citizens feel it has cleaned up their part of town and it has become safer. Because it is legal, taggers, or graffiti artists, have more time to develop their works of art. No longer do they need to do it under the cover of night or do it quickly in fear of getting arrested. This luxury of time helps the artists develop more in-depth pieces of art. These public graffiti walls have become so well known around the world that people go there specifically to see the newest developments. It has even become a tourist spot of sorts.

depth	critics	control
citizens	luxury	

1 Most _____ like the designated areas for graffiti.

2 The graffiti artists now have the _____ to take their time when they paint.

3 The city officials have some _____ over where and how much graffiti is in a city by designating certain walls for graffiti.

4 Some _____ of legalized graffiti say that it takes away their freedom of expression.

5 Some graffiti art lacked _____ , because artists were rushing in fear of getting arrested.

ANSWER KEY

PRE-TEST

Part 1 pp. 1–2
1. d, 2. c, 3. b, 4. b, 5. c

Part 2 p. 3
Main Idea: 3
Supporting Details: 1, 2, 4

Part 3 p. 4
1. b, 2. c

Part 4 p. 5
1. a, 2. c

Part 5 p. 6
1. c, 2. b, 3. a

Part 6 p. 7
1. d, 2. d, 3. b

Part 7 p. 7
1. a, 2. b

Part 8 p. 7
1. b, 2. b

Part 9 p. 8
Subjects: All I, forecast
Verbs: sat, see, worry, called

Part 10 p. 8
Subject Pronouns: we, She, she, She, I,
she, they, I, we, I, I
Object Pronouns: her, it, them, them, her, me
Possessive Adjectives: My, our, My, her,
Their, my

Part 11 p. 9
1. those, 2. This, 3. These, 4. that

Part 12 p. 9
b

Part 13 p. 9
1. d, 2. a, 3. d

Part 14 p. 10
1. burned out
2. cut back
3. barely
4. downside

5. involved
6. cut down

COMPREHENSION SKILLS
Previewing and Predicting

PREVIEWING

Practice 1 p. 11
1. a, 2. c, 3. a, 4. c

Practice 2

Part 1 p. 12
1. b, 2. c, 3. b

Part 2 p. 13
4. c, 5. b, 6. c

Part 3 p. 13
7. c, 8. a, 9. c

Practice 3

Part 1 p. 14
d

Part 2 p. 15
d

Part 3 p. 15
b

PREDICTING

Practice 1 p. 16
1. c, 2. d, 3. b, 4. b

Practice 2

Part 1 p. 17
Ideas in the article: c, d, f, h
Ideas not in the article: a, b, e, g

Part 2 p. 18
Ideas in the article: c, d, e, g
Ideas not in the article: a, b, f, h

Part 3 p. 19
Ideas in the article: b, e, f, g
Ideas not in the article: a, c, d, h

Practice 3 pp. 20–21

1. c, 2. b, 3. d, 4. b

COMBINED SKILLS: PREVIEWING AND PREDICTING

Practice 1 pp. 22–23

1. a, 2. d, 3. c, 4. d, 5. b, 6. a, 7. b, 8. c

Practice 2

Part 1 p. 24

a, b, d, e

Part 2 p. 25

a, b, c, d

Part 3 p. 26

a, b, c, d, e, f

Identifying Topics, Main Ideas, and Details

IDENTIFYING THE TOPIC OF A LIST

Practice 1 p. 27

1. e, 2. f, 3. d, 4. c, 5. g, 6. d

Practice 2 p. 27

1. dictionary
2. meat
3. education
4. beverage
5. town
6. plant

UNDERSTANDING PARAGRAPHS

Practice 1 pp. 28–29

1. a, 2. b, 3. a, 4. b, 5. a

Practice 2 p. 29

1. a, 2. b, 3. a, 4. a, 5. b

Practice 3

Part 1 pp. 30–31

Topic Sentence: 7
Body Sentences: 1, 2, 3, 4, 5
Concluding Sentence: 6

Part 2 p. 31

Topic Sentence: 4
Body Sentences: 1, 3, 5, 6, 7
Concluding Sentence: 2

Part 3 p. 32

Topic Sentence: 1
Body Sentences: 2, 4, 5
Concluding Sentence: 3

IDENTIFYING THE TOPIC OF A PARAGRAPH

Practice 1 pp. 33–34

1. d, 2. a, 3. b, 4. b

Practice 2 pp. 34–35

1. d, 2. a, 3. d, 4. a

IDENTIFYING THE MAIN IDEA

Practice 1 pp. 35–36

1. d, 2. b, 3. b, 4. a

Practice 2 p. 37

1. Animals that help others are called service animals.
2. Guide dogs help people who cannot see well.
3. Hearing dogs are dogs that help people who don't hear well.
4. These animals provide emotional support for people who are sick, depressed, or lonely.
5. The Capuchin monkey can help people who are paralyzed or have other problems with walking or moving.
6. The organizations that train these service animals also make sure that they are leading rewarding, enjoyable, healthy lives.

Practice 3 pp. 38–39

1
Main Idea: A
Too Specific: C
Too General: B

2
Main Idea: C
Too Specific: B
Too General: A

IDENTIFYING SUPPORTING DETAILS

Practice 1

Part 1 p. 40

Main Idea: 1

Supporting Details: 2, 3, 4

Part 2 p. 40

Main Idea: 1

Supporting Details: 2, 3, 4

Part 3 p. 41

Main Idea: 3

Supporting Details: 1, 2, 4

Part 4 p. 42

Main Idea: 1

Supporting Details: 2, 3, 4

Part 5 p. 42

Main Idea: 4

Supporting Details: 1, 2, 3

Practice 2 p. 43

1

He creates games and activities to help us to review the material we learn in class.

He lets us work in groups.

We also take a lot of field trips.

2

Some superstitions relate to animals.

Others have to do with things.

Certain numbers and calendar days are superstitious for some people.

3

Other passengers, especially children, can be very distracting to our driving.

Another big distraction is your cell phone.

Food can also be a distraction.

4

The Thai people use Bird's Eye chili peppers in many dishes.

Before you try a spoonful of Sichuan Hot-Pot, make sure you have a towel around to wipe your face!

Vindaloo Pork has a very hot curry sauce that will definitely make you reach for some water!

Scanning

SCANNING FOR KEY WORDS AND PHRASES

Practice 1 pp. 44–45

1. a, c, f
2. d, f, h
3. b, d, g
4. a, d, g
5. b, d, f
6. a, e, g
7. c, f, g
8. a, e, h

Practice 2 pp. 45–46

1. a, d, e, h
2. a, d, e, h
3. a, c, f, h
4. c, e, g, h
5. a, d, f, h
6. b, d, f, g

Practice 3 pp. 46–47

1. b, 2. b, 3. d, 4. c, 5. a

SCANNING FOR INFORMATION

Practice 1 pp. 48–49

1. d, 2. c, 3. b, 4. d, 5. b, 6. c

Practice 2 p. 50

1. b, 2. d, 3. b, 4. c, 5. b, 6. c

Practice 3 p. 51

1. a, 2. c, 3. b, 4. d, 5. c

Practice 4 p. 52

1. c, 2. d, 3. c, 4. b, 5. b, 6. a

Making Inferences

MAKING INFERENCES FROM CONVERSATIONS

Practice 1 p. 54
1. b, 2. a, 3. c, 4. a, 5. a

Practice 2 p. 55
1. c, 2. a, 3. a, 4. a, 5. b, 6. b

Practice 3 pp. 56–57
1. a, 2. b, 3. a, 4. d, 5. d

MAKING INFERENCES IN FICTION

Practice 1 pp. 57–59
1. b, 2. d, 3. a, 4. c, 5. d, 6. a, 7. a, 8. c

Practice 2 pp. 59–60
1. a, 2. b, 3. d, 4. c, 5. b, 6. c, 7. d, 8. c

Practice 3 pp. 60–62
1. b, 2. a, 3. c, 4. b, 5. a, 6. c, 7. a, 8. d

THINKING IN ENGLISH

Practice 1 p. 63
1. a, 2. a, 3. a, 4. b, 5. d, 6. a, 7. a, 8. b

Practice 2 pp. 64–65
1. a, 2. a, 3. c, 4. b, 5. b, 6. d, 7. a, 8. a

Recognizing Patterns

LISTING PATTERN

Practice 1 pp. 66–67
1. many, One, Another, yet another, last, a few
2. also, a lot of, One, another, Other, For example, many
3. Many, several, First, Also, Last
4. many, One, Other, In addition, One

Practice 2

Part 1 p. 67
Category A: 2
Category B: 1, 3

Part 2 p. 68
Category A: 2
Category B: 1, 3, 4

Part 3 pp. 68–69
Category A: 3
Category B: 1, 2, 4

SEQUENCE PATTERN

Practice 1 pp. 70–71
1. 1849, Soon, A few years later, When, at last
2. After, When, as soon as
3. first, At that time
4. When, One day, next day, As soon as
5. 1856, Soon, After, Every, Each time
6. After, Soon, Soon after

Practice 2 pp. 71–72
Main Idea Sentence with Signal Word stating a sequence: 3, 5

Supporting Detail Sentences with Signal Words that list steps: 1, 2, 4, 6, 7, 8, 9, 10, 11, 12

COMPARISON PATTERN

Practice 1 p. 74
1. different, too, but, however, different, on the other hand, different
2. After, different, differ, However, difference, unlike, but, differences
3. different, both, but, different, differ, more than, while, but, unlike, whereas, differences, differences
4. Both, alike, similar, Both, both, too, similarity, both

Practice 2 pp. 75–76
Main Idea Sentence with Signal Word stating a comparison:
3, 7

Supporting Detail Sentences with Signal Words that show similarity: 1, 4, 9

Supporting Detail Sentences with Signal

Words that show differences: 2, 5, 6, 8
Supporting Detail Sentences with Signal
Words that show comparison: 10, 11

Identifying Patterns

Practice 1 pp. 77–78

1. a, 2. b, 3. c, 4. a

Practice 2 pp. 78–79

1. a, 2. b, 3. c, 4. a

Comprehension Skills Practice Test

Part 1   Previewing p. 80

1. c, 2. d, 3. b, 4. d

Part 2   Predicting pp. 81–83

1

Ideas in the book: 2, 3, 5

Not ideas in the book: 1, 4, 6, 7

2

Ideas in the article: 1, 3, 7, 8

Not ideas in the article: 2, 4, 5, 6

3

Ideas in the book: 1, 3, 5, 6

Not ideas in the book: 2, 4, 7, 8

Part 3   Previewing and Predicting p. 84

1. c, 2. a, 3. b, 4. d, 5. a, 6. b

Part 4   Identifying Topics, Main Ideas, and Details pp. 84–85

1. a, 2. b

Part 5   Identifying Topics, Main Ideas, and Details p. 85

Topic Sentence: 1

Body Sentences: 3, 4, 5, 6, 7

Concluding Sentences: 2

Part 6   Identifying the Topic of a Paragraph p. 86

1. c, 2. b

Part 7   Identifying the Main Idea p. 87

1. One of the most beautiful places to visit is Hawaii.

2. Kauai is known for its dramatic and natural beauty.

3. Oahu is the state capital and home to the majority of Hawaii's population.

4. Maui has many stunning beaches that are every color, including white, red, and black.

5. Hawaii, also known as the Big Island, is the largest of all the islands.

6. If you want a little bit of everything, it is easy to travel from one island to the next, so you don't have to choose just one to visit.

Part 8   Supporting Details p. 88

1

Main Idea: 1

Supporting Details: 2, 3, 4, 5

2

Main Idea: 3

Supporting Details: 1, 2, 4

Part 9   Scanning for Information p. 89

1. b, 2. d, 3. b, 4. b, 5. d, 6. b

Part 10   Making Inferences from Dialogues pp. 90–91

1. c, 2. a, 3. c, 4. d, 5. a

Part 11   Making Inferences in Fiction pp. 91–92

1. b, 2. c, 3. d, 4. a, 5. c

Part 12   Thinking in English pp. 92–93

1. b, 2. a, 3. b, 4. d, 5. a

Part 13   Identifying Patterns of Organization pp. 93–94

1. b, 2. a, 3. c

VOCABULARY BUILDING
Dictionary Work
USING GUIDEWORDS

Practice 1 p. 96

1. a, d, e

2. b, c, f

3. a, d, e

4. b, d, e

5. a, b, e

6. b, c, e

Practice 2 p. 96

cold/color

colony

collect

collide

collar

comedian/command

comfort

comma

comic

comedy

colorful/come

coma

colt

combination

column

PARTS OF SPEECH

Practice 1 pp. 97–98

1. d, 2. a, 3. b, 4. c, 5. a, 6. a, 7. c, 8. b

Practice 2 p. 99

Verb

crowded

coach

vacation

drop

Adjective

neat

friendly

crowded

anxious

Adverb

successfully

overly

increasingly

comfortably

Noun

imagination

taste

vacation

coach

FINDING THE RIGHT MEANING

Practice 1 pp. 100–101

1. b, 2. a, 3. a, 4. b, 5. a, 6. b, 7. b, 8. a

Practice 2 p. 101

1. bus

2. color

3. exit

4. march

5. light

6. sight

7. program

8. market

Word Parts

ROOTS, PREFIXES, AND SUFFIXES

Practice 1 pp. 102–103

1. Prefix: dis
   Meaning: not

2. Prefix: anti
   Meaning: opposite

3. Prefix: ir
   Meaning: not

4. Prefix: im
   Meaning: not

5. Prefix: re
   Meaning: again

6. Prefix: multi
   Meaning: many

Practice 2 p. 103

1. b, 2. c, 3. d, 4. a, 5. b, 6. c

Practice 3 pp. 103–104

1. a, 2. c, 3. d, 4. b, 5. a, 6. b

Practice 4 p. 104

1. b, c

2. a, b, c

3. c

4. a, b, c

5. a, c

6. b, c

7. a, c

8. a, b, c

WORD FORMS AND FAMILIES

Practice 1 p. 105

1. a adjective
   b noun
   c adverb

2. a noun
   b adjective
   c adverb

3. a adverb
   b noun
   c adjective

4. a adverb
   b adjective
   c noun

5. a adjective
   b noun
   c adverb

6. a verb
   b noun
   c adverb

7. a noun
   b verb
   c adverb

8. a noun
   b adjective
   c adverb

Practice 2 p. 106

Noun

destruction, promotion, injection, reflection, information, permanence, beauty

Adjective

beautiful, decisive, informative, amusing, destructive, reflective, permanent

Verb

destroy, inject, inform, decide, reflect, promote, amuse

Practice 3 p. 107

1. a, 2. c, 3. b, 4. c, 5. a, 6. b, 7. a, 8. b, 9. c

Practice 4 p. 109

1. a, 2. b, 3. a, 4. b, 5. a, 6. b, 7. a, 8. b, 9. a, 10. b, 11. a, 12. b

Practice 5 p. 110

1. a, 2. b, 3. b, 4. a, 5. a, 6. b, 7. b, 8. a, 9. a, 10. b

-ED AND -ING ADJECTIVES

Practice 1 p. 111

1. tiring, tired

2. excited, exciting

3. annoying, annoyed

4. embarrassing, embarrassed

5. relaxed, relaxing

6. interested, interesting

Practice 2 p. 112

1. shocked

2. satisfied

3. surprised

4. satisfying

5. shocking

6. frightening

7. worried

Guessing Meaning from Context

WHAT IS CONTEXT?

Practice 1 p. 113

1. began

2. head

3. champion

4. met

5. immediately

6. competitive

Practice 2 p. 114

1. passed easily from one person to another
2. clothes
3. physical strength
4. people in my life are making it difficult to get anything done
5. extremely overweight
6. repeats the first sound of every word

Practice 3 pp. 114–115

1. c, 2. a, 3. c, 4. d, 5. b, 6. c, 7. d, 8. a

GUESSING THE MEANING OF WORDS AND PHRASES

Practice 1 pp. 116–117

1. b, 2. a, 3. c, 4. a, 5. b, 6. a

Practice 2 pp. 117–118

1. a, 2. c, 3. c, 4. a, 5. c, 6. a

Practice 3 p. 118

1. to run faster or farther
2. behaving in a very excited way
3. always do something
4. to do something to an extreme
5. to want or need something very badly
6. very happy

Practice 4 p. 119

1. strong
2. do what they are supposed to do
3. to give time or money
4. to meet
5. to end someone's work contract
6. funny

Practice 5 p. 120

1. d, 2. b, 3. c, 4. b, 5. c, 6. a

Practice 6 p. 121

1. a, 2. d, 3. c, 4. a, 5. a, 6. a

Practice 7 p. 122

1. learn new things
2. always doing something
3. faint and fall

4. overwhelmed
5. to talk to
6. very different from one another

Practice 8 p. 123

1. to be nervous or anxious
2. to not have any more time
3. to have a rest
4. to talk to regularly
5. to look like or act like
6. to invent

Phrases and Collocations

COMMON TYPES OF PHRASES

Practice 1 pp. 124–125

1. a, 2. c, 3. c, 4. c, 5. b, 6. b

Practice 2 p. 125

1. get over
2. keep an eye an
3. give me a hand
4. now and then
5. run out of money
6. break the record

Practice 3 p. 126

1. a, 2. b, 3. b, 4. a, 5. a, 6. a, 7. a, 8. b, 9. a, 10. a

PHRASES IN CONTEXT

Practice 1 pp. 127–128

1. spends money
2. do our best
3. get a haircut
4. have lunch
5. break the rules
6. makes a difference
7. make a noise
8. day in and day out

Practice 2 pp. 128–129

1. c
2. a
3. b

4. a

5. a

6. a

7. c

8. a

Practice 3 p. 130

1. waste time

2. come out

3. turn up

4. get through

5. be right back

6. save people's lives

7. hold my friend's place

8. catch fire

Practice 4 p. 130

Many doctors agree on one thing: sleep is important! Sleep research shows that if you take a rest every day, you won't get sick. If you don't get enough sleep, then your body will pay the price. The average amount of sleep needed is 7–8 hours a night. This sleep may seem like a waste of time, but you need it!

Not only is a proper night's sleep important, but resting for 15 minutes every day can make a difference in how you feel, also. In Spain, the Spaniards take a rest, called a siesta. After they have lunch every day, they lie down for about 30 to 60 minutes. After their siesta, they feel rested and ready for work. When they go back to work they feel that their brain got a rest and they are back on track.

Be sure to take time to get a good night's sleep and a rest every day. As time passes, you will begin to feel healthier and happier and you will have more energy.

Practice 5 p. 131

Did you get a cut? Burn yourself? If you have a problem, chances are there may be a solution right in your very own kitchen. If you are cooking and you get a cut, don't worry and don't waste time getting a bandage. Your home remedy is right in the kitchen. Get some black pepper and pour it on your cut. Within a few seconds, the bleeding will stop! One man said that after cutting his finger, he put some pepper on it, and the bleeding stopped immediately. His wife got frightened and took him to the hospital. After the nurse took a look at the pepper, she washed it off and the bleeding started again! The man got fed up, walked out of the hospital, and went straight home to get more pepper!

There are many more remedies like the ones here in this article. With these ideas you will not only save money and save time, you will also save yourself the trouble of going to the hospital!

How Words Work in Sentences

IDENTIFYING PARTS OF A SENTENCE

Practice 1 pp. 132–133
Subjects
television
house
fire
people
money
information
skiing
university
Verbs
gave
is
work
buys
stands
grew
provides
fell

Practice 2 p. 133

1. Subject: friend
   Verb: works
2. Subject: shelter
   Verb: receives
3. Subject: animals
   Verb: are
4. Subject: animal
   Verb: comes
5. Subject: work
   Verb: is
6. Subject: employees
   Verb: care
7. Subject: shelters
   Verb: euthanize
8. Subject: shelter
   Verb: is
9. Subject: She
   Verb: enjoys
10. Subject: People
    Verb: make

PERSONAL PRONOUNS AND POSSESSIVE ADJECTIVES

Practice 1 pp. 134–135

1. He, We, I, He
2. They, they, they, They
3. She, she, She, she
4. He, He, he, I
5. We, we, I, We
6. They, It, They, We

Practice 2 p. 135

1. me
2. me, her, them, them, them, me, her, it, it, her, him, him, him
3. her, us, her, them
4. her

Practice 3 p. 136

1. My
2. My, his, its

3. My, her, Her, their
4. Our, Its, our, Their
5. your, their

Practice 4 pp. 136–137

Subject Pronouns

He
She
It
They
You

Possessive Adjectives

its
their
his

Object Pronouns

it
them
him

DEMONSTRATIVE PRONOUNS AND ADJECTIVES; REFERENTS

Practice 1 p. 138

1. These
2. Those
3. That, These
4. This
5. These

Practice 2 p. 139

1. Those
2. This
3. these
4. That
5. That support
6. this reason

Practice 3 pp. 140–141

1. street vendors
2. to not dive in the shallow area of the pool
3. a great jazz band that played music

4. beautiful yellow irises from Japan

5. my years of living in Paris

6. from cookies and cakes to pies and donuts

Practice 4 p. 141

1. many women's suffrage groups

2. There were some supporters who were more extreme in their ways

3. They often threatened women's lives, disrupted their speeches, and destroyed their signs; the supporters

4. women were able to vote in all elections

5. There were many brave women who were the first to be elected officials of the United States government

VOCABULARY BUILDING PRACTICE TEST

Part 1 p. 142

1. a, d, e

2. b, c, f

Part 2 p. 142

1. d, 2. a, 3. b, 4. c

Part 3 p. 143

1. fall

2. garden

3. fit

4. windy

Part 4 p. 143

1. Prefix: trans

   Meaning: between two things

2. Prefix: dis

   Meaning: not

3. Prefix: ex

   Meaning: no longer doing/being

4. Prefix: sub

   Meaning: under

5. Prefix: pre

   Meaning: before

Part 5 p. 143

1. a noun

   b verb

   c adverb

   d adjective

2. a noun

   b verb

   c adjective

Part 6 p. 144

1. annoying

2. confusing

3. interested

4. amazed

5. annoyed

6. interesting

7. confused

Part 7 p. 144

1. b, 2. a, 3. c

Part 8 p. 145

1. to agree with someone

2. wait to make a decision

3. the best of both choices

4. very rarely

Part 9 p. 145

1. c, 2. b, 3. b

Part 10 pp. 145–146

Fire is dangerous and should never be played with. In an instant, your whole life can change if a fire gets out of control. There are many reasons for house fires. A curtain that is too close to a candle can catch fire instantaneously and before you know it, your house is burned to the ground. Cigarettes are often the reason for house fires. Many people fall asleep while smoking a cigarette. The cigarette drops on the ground or in your bed, and there is little you can do to stop the fire from taking over. The firefighters will try to save your life, but often it is too late. Even if you are very careful with fire hazards in your house, it is always a good idea to make a plan just in case a house fire breaks out. As a family, decide on a <u>meeting place</u>. This could be your neighbor's house or a big tree in your yard. Wherever you choose to meet, the important thing is to just <u>get out</u> as <u>quickly as you can</u>.

Part 11 p. 146

1. that
2. this
3. Those
4. these

Part 12 p. 146

1. The paintings
2. the desserts
3. learning about the rocks and gems
4. blogs or sites written by other people

READING FASTER

READING FASTER PRACTICE P. 149

1. c, 2. b, 3. c, 4. a, 5. b, 6. b

TIMED READING PRACTICE

Practice 1

Timed Reading 1 p. 151

1. c, 2. c, 3. b, 4. a, 5. b, 6. d

Timed Reading 2 p. 153

1. c, 2. a, 3. c, 4. a, 5. a, 6. b, 7. d, 8. d

Practice 2

Timed Reading 1 p. 155

1. c, 2. b, 3. a, 4. d, 5. b, 6. a

Timed Reading 2 p. 157

1. c, 2. d, 3. a, 4. a, 5. d, 6. b, 7. a, 8. c

Practice 3

Timed Reading 1 p. 159

1. a, 2. d, 3. c, 4. c, 5. b, 6. b

Timed Reading 2 p. 161

1. a, 2. a, 3. c, 4. d, 5. b, 6. d

STUDY SKILLS
Choosing Words to Learn

Practice 1 p. 163

Answers will vary.

Practice 2 p. 164

Answers will vary.

Practice 3 p. 165

Answers will vary.

Practice 4 p. 166

Answers will vary.

Practice 5 p. 167

Answers will vary.

Storing and Studying New Words

VOCABULARY NOTEBOOKS

Practice 1 p. 169

Answers will vary.

Practice 2 p. 170

Answers will vary.

Practice 3 p. 171

Answers will vary.

WORD MAPS

Practice 1 p. 173

Answers will vary.

Practice 2 p. 174

Answers will vary.

Practice 3 p. 175

Answers will vary.

WORD CARDS

Practice 1 p. 177

Answers will vary.

Practice 2 p. 178

Answers will vary.

Practice 3 p. 179

Answers will vary.

LANGUAGE IN CONTEXT

Practice 1

Part 1 p. 180

ever, sound, something, Most, likely, birds, second, allow, change, reach, second

Part 2 p. 180

1. false, 2. true, 3. true, 4. false, 5. false

Part 3 p. 181

1. b, 2. c, 3. b, 4. d, 5. a

Part 4 p. 182

1. allow	6. second
2. flap	7. reach
3. zoom	8. direction
4. sound	9. beak
5. buzzing	10. likely

Practice 2

Part 1 p. 183

trouble, day, enough, sleep, Doctors, people, between, sleep, night, Begin, particular, sleep, Sleep

Part 2 p. 183

1. false, 2. false, 3. false, 4. true, 5. false

Part 3 p. 184

1. a, 2. c, 3. b, 4. a, 5. c

Part 4 p. 185

1. focusing
2. routine
3. difficulty
4. mentally
5. recommend
6. healthy
7. physically
8. enough
9. per

Practice 3

Part 1 p. 186

love, dogs, horses, animals, love, back, help, many, Animals, help, service, animals, animals, help, able, alone, Service, animals, animals, human, human

Part 2 p. 186

1. false, 2. true, 3. true, 4. false, 5. true

Part 3 p. 187

1. c, 2. b, 3. d, 4. a, 5. b

Part 4 p. 188

1. tasks
2. service
3. laws
4. human
5. alone
6. back
7. pets
8. state

Practice 4

Part 1 p. 189

Today, develop, learn, provide, opportunities, learn, important, life, school, stay, gain

Part 2 p. 189

1. false, 2. true, 3. true, 4. false, 5. true, 6. true

Part 3 p. 190

1. b, 2. d, 3. d, 4. a, 5. b

Part 4 p. 191

1. activities
2. gain
3. develop
4. educational
5. talents
6. provide
7. opportunities
8. teamwork

Practice 5

Part 1 p. 192

people, news, several, reasons, First, look, newspaper, Again, people, already, work, newspaper, Last, current, news, people, information, newspaper, news, reasons, people, news

Part 2 p. 192

1. true, 2. false, 3. true, 4. true, 5. true

Part 3 pp. 193–194

1. a, 2. c, 3. b, 4. d, 5. a, 6. b, 7. a, 8. c

Part 4 p. 194

1. several
2. current
3. nowadays
4. capabilities
5. convenient
6. primary
7. update
8. additional

Practice 6

Part 1 p. 195

Before, coins, paper, things, money, popular, such, since, food, such, since, food, things, such, money, example, money, Since, today, money

Part 2 p. 195

1. true, 2. true, 3. false, 4. true, 5. false, 6. false, 7. true, 8. false

Part 3 pp. 196–197

1. b, 2. c, 3. d, 4. b, 5. d, 6. a, 7. b, 8. d

Part 4 p. 197

1. necessary
2. rich
3. frivolous
4. popular
5. survival
6. decorations
7. currency
8. nonetheless

POST-TEST

Part 1 pp. 207–208

1. c, 2. f, 3. a, 4. b, 5. c

Part 2 p. 209

Main Idea: 5
Supporting Details: 1, 2, 3, 4, 6, 7, 8

Part 3 p. 210

1. b, 2. c

Part 4 p. 211

1. a, 2. c

Part 5 pp. 211–212

1. c, 2. b, 3. a

Part 6 p. 212

1. b, 2. d, 3. a

Part 7 p. 213

1. a, 2. c

Part 8 p. 213

1. a, 2. c

Part 9 p. 214

Subjects: schools, data, principal
Verbs: contract, inform, contacted

Part 10 p. 214

Subject Pronouns: we, She, it, She, They, She, She, they, I, they, We, Everybody, That

Object Pronouns: all, most, it, her, him, me, it, us, us

Possessive Adjectives: My, My, her, Our, My, Their, my, her, My, His

Part 11 p. 215

1. this, 2. those, 3. that, 4. these

Part 12 p. 215

b

Part 13 pp. 215–216

1. d, 2. a, 3. d

Part 14 p. 216

1. citizens
2. luxury
3. control
4. critics
5. depth